The Long Overdue Library Book: Stories Librarians Tell Each Other

Sandy Bradley and Elsa Pendleton

ISBN:1490572430
ISBN-13:978-1490572437

Introduction

Not everybody wants to be a librarian.

This is something librarians find difficult to understand. Of course there can be problems: the mother just back from the pediatrician, whose three children have been diagnosed with chicken pox, can she please have extra books? being accosted in the supermarket parking lot by a man with a stack of overdue books; the evening and weekend shifts; the stereotyping. Oh yes the stereotyping. **Shhhhhh**.

But there are pleasures as well. Children's hugs at the end of story hour. Tracking down the correct answer to a reference question. Coaxing a non-reader into a Lemony Snicket book and seeing him return the next day for another one. Librarians like to share these experiences with each other, and enjoy telling their stories.

These stories, like libraries themselves, have changed over the decades. For those not fortunate to have witnessed these changes, welcome to the world of the true, devoted, book-loving Librarian. Our hope is to provide some interesting information and a chuckle or two. **Enjoy!**

Contents

Section 1:

The Library Experience

Denver, CO Main Library Entrance – J. Bradley

There it is: that wonderful library smell. How could I have forgotten it? The feel of libraries – the way they look, smell, sound – lingers intensely as the memories of a fierce first love.

Susan Allen Toth, *Reading Rooms*

CHAPTER 1 - **FEELINGS**

There is a special feel about a library.

I first experienced this at about the age of six when I was allowed to choose several books by myself from the public library.

Of course, my sisters and I were not allowed to check them out all by ourselves. Back then you had to be able to sign your own name, in cursive, to your library card application. The public schools didn't teach cursive until the third grade. It was a large hurdle for me, someone with poor hand-eye coordination.

When I did manage to get my own card, the world became much bigger and brighter for me. I carried my card with me, in my small purse, wherever I went.

When summer rolled around, the library was my happiest place to be. I could walk to the library, (which seemed far away, past all the houses, the bus stop, and the drug store) and choose the ten books that I was allowed to check out on my card. When I finished reading them all, I would return them and get ten new ones.

I enjoyed other parts of the summer, sleeping late, swimming, camping, but nothing was as wonderful as the long hot afternoons curled up with *Charlotte's Web*, *Freddy the Detective*, *The Black Stallion*, *Tom Sawyer*, *Caddie Woodlawn*, *The Secret Garden*—there seemed to be no end to the deliciousness.

I noticed that each time I returned books to the library, I felt a sense of wonder and excitement. How would I choose the next books? What new characters would I become friends with, what new places would I explore?

I usually started with the authors I already knew, and browsed the rows for titles by them. But new titles could entice me. I would open the pages and look for the liner notes that were pasted into the book. (At that time, book jackets were routinely removed from the books prior to processing them and before putting them on the shelf). If someone had the time and enough glue, the liner notes were carefully removed and glued to the inside of the book. That was a way to get a feel for the book. Otherwise, you had to scan some pages to see if it seemed promising.

As I grew older and my school began to make demands upon me, it became clear that my little storefront branch library was not sufficient. I ventured farther away to the larger regional branch.

The building was huge and airy, and there were many rooms. Instead of a small alcove for children's books, this library had an entire room. There were shelves of current magazines, and archives of older issues that you could ask to see. Instead of a few reference books closely guarded behind the desk, there were many rows of books, which you were allowed to pull down and use by yourself.

The experience was like my first visit to a library, but intensified.

Then, when I entered high school. I needed special sources for my term papers and even the regional library lacked them.

The main library was located downtown and it amazed me. There was a single room just to hold all the card catalogs!

NOTE: For those unfamiliar with the pre-computer days, cards with information about the books were kept in lovely wooden cabinets. The cards were organized by author, title, and subject to help readers locate the books on the shelves.

When I found the art history books that I needed there was an entire room devoted to them. One room held nothing but newspapers and magazines. I didn't even have time to explore the entire building.

But again, I had that special feeling, that the entire world could be yours if you could master the system and use it for yourself. It felt very selfish, but uniquely satisfying to know that it was possible to find what I wanted, if not in this library, in another, and it all belonged to me.

Later in life I worked in a variety of libraries of different types, technical, academic, and public. Each gave me a sense of well-being. It didn't matter what type of task I was given, I felt at home, and satisfied.

Much of the satisfaction came from the belief that I was helping others. If I put the call number on a book, or filed a catalog card, I was helping people find it on the shelf. If I helped a patron find a book on a shelf I was helping that person. They might need that book to do their job, improve themselves, pass a class, or pass the time. That sense of purpose added to my belief that a library was a great place to be.

When I travel, I love to visit other libraries, however big or small. Yes, I know it is a busman's holiday, but each one is unique and has something new to offer me.

Each one still reawakens my feeling that within the walls are wonderful treasures to be uncovered. It doesn't matter if the library in question is as large as the Library of Congress or as small as a shelf set on a cruise ship, it is a library, and I want to visit it. I want to experience again that wonderful feeling that there are good things in the world, available to all. I get my fix!

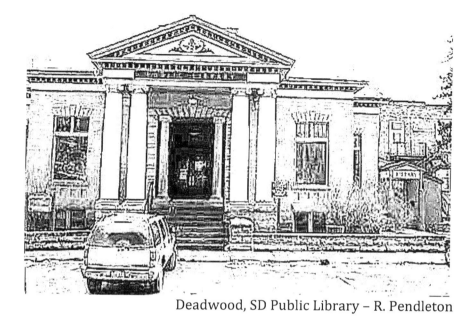

Deadwood, SD Public Library – R. Pendleton

As a child, my number one best friend was the librarian in my grade school. I actually believed all those books belonged to her.

Erma Bombeck

CHAPTER 2 - **FIRST MEMORY**

When I re-play my first library memory, I see myself, about 10 years old, entering the library of the elementary school I just started attending. I asked, "Why are we were going to the library?" I didn't understand the concept! The library was tiny, but I was awed by seeing so many books. I asked, "Where are the books I am allowed to check out?" My teacher said. "You can check out any books you want."

I was overwhelmed. Up until that day I had saved my allowance to buy one book at a time from the dime store. Now I didn't even know where to begin. I decided to pick a spot along the back wall of the room to start browsing, then work my way around the walls and through the stacks as we returned each week.

I can still picture (and smell) the books I checked out that first day. One was *A Rocket in My Pocket* (1948), a book of children's rhymes collected by Carl Withers, and the other was *Dr. Tom Dooley: My Story* (1958). Dooley's book about his service to the people in Vietnam in the 1950's first opened my eyes to the world around me.

The next week I went back to the same shelf to find out more about the world, and found *Hiroshima* (1954) by John Hersey. I could not believe that no one had told me about this horrific event. I realized I had a lot to learn, and fortunately, I had figured out how to do it.

Outside the Franklin, MA Public Library – R. Pendleton

I had always thought of paradise in form and image as a library.

Jorge Luis Borges

CHAPTER 3 - **MY LIBRARY**

My library and I are old friends; I think of it as mine for many reasons. In recent years this is because I support it - willingly - with my taxes. But for several years after high school it was a second home, located just 20 feet from where I worked. While taking breaks, or during lunch, I ate - and smoked - quickly, spending what time remained discovering its riches.

Much of the work done by myself and those who worked with me was for the benefit of local agencies, with the library conveniently receiving custom made shelving, wood signage and help with repairs and maintenance. Such contact inevitably led to close relationships with the staff, most notably the County Librarian, who, along with her husband, soon became close family friends.

Relationships evolved, smoking became chewing tobacco, and my wife and I were married in the County Librarian's back yard. Children followed, a brother died from cancer, with my nicotine habit being put to rest as well. The County Librarian eventually retired, my workplace changed, with the relationship to my library changing also. Children's overdue book charges began augmenting the support provided by taxation, with previous excursions in search of knowledge and escape being replaced by a pilgrimage of reparations for enjoying the same.

Over the years I've found my library to be many things: a source of information, facts and fantasy, a place to meet old friends and make new ones, and shelter from the realities of an all too often, indifferent world. The secrets of the Dewey Decimal System, however, continue to elude me.

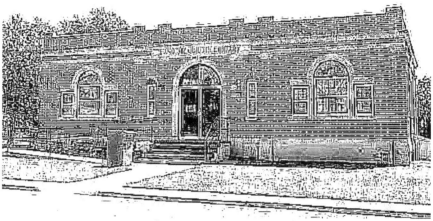
Wilson, KS, Lang Memorial Library – R. Pendleton

Most homes valued at over $250,000 have a library.
That should tell us something.

Jim Rohn (*Jim Rohn's Weekly E-zine* – Jan. 27, 2004)

CHAPTER 4 – **ON THE SHELVES**

Shuffling through other people's houses and peering at their bookshelves may not be everyone's idea of a fun Saturday — but it did appeal to me, and to my 23-year-old son, and to a surprising number of other people who showed up for a recent tour of private libraries in Concord. The streets in front of the participating houses were lined with parked cars; the doorsteps were scattered with shoes; and the rooms were thronged with people in stockinged feet pausing in front of the shelves, silently scanning titles or whispering to a companion, "I have that," or "Oh, Alice Munro — I love Alice Munro."

In the course of the afternoon, we saw libraries that were studies where people worked, libraries that were big sitting rooms lined with books, libraries in hallways and dining rooms and family rooms, libraries that meandered and libraries that soared. We saw a serene self-contained cottage — you walked out of the main house and across an apple orchard to get to it — furnished with a piano, a sofa, and a big wall of books.

 We saw a rich, dark, quiet library housed in what had once been a three-car garage. We saw a lot more libraries than we did houses, since virtually every house had more than one room that was filled with books and open to the public. And then there were the closed doors and politely cordoned-off staircases, and the sense that beyond those barriers were other private rooms filled with more books - bedside tables that must be piled with recent fiction, guest room shelves stuffed with junky mysteries, kids' rooms lined with Harry Potter or, if the kids were kids a long time ago, maybe Tom Swift and Arthur Ransome and Daddy-Long-Legs.

In some ways, the library tour was weird and awkward, and it should not have worked. Reading, after all, is a solitary activity. It's between you and the book, and no one in the crowd of visitors touched a book in any of those libraries. So what was the appeal?

Well, snooping was part of it. Just as a garden tour lets you walk through backyards that are hidden from the street, a library tour invites you to look into physical and psychological spaces that are ordinarily private - not just the actual rooms that hold the books, but the minds and souls of the people who have assembled the collections. We saw bound sets of Thackeray and Victor Hugo inherited from parents and grandparents. We saw Stieg Larsson nestled in with esoteric volumes on the history of philosophy. In a house packed with books on every conceivable subject, we saw one shelf whose height and contents clearly, enticingly, said, "Grandchild, this is yours." And in all the houses we saw the deep, passionate collections that reflect the individual interests - and professional careers - of their owners, historians and biographers, legal and medical scholars, publishers.

Talking in the car as we drove from house to house, my son and I agreed that one of the day's big pleasures was spotting a quirky personal favorite — Guy Sajer's *The Forgotten Soldier,* or John Marquand's biography of Newburyport eccentric Lord Timothy Dexter — on a stranger's shelf. We also agreed that we couldn't wait to get home to look at all our own books again.

I get angry and discouraged whenever I see a story predicting — or worse, recommending — the demise of the printed book. Electronic content is more efficient, more economical, and more compact, such stories argue. What I would argue back is: A book is more than just content. It is heft; smell; design; typeface; the texture, weight, and color of the paper; the sticker on the back cover from the bookstore in France where you bought it; the wrinkled pages that remind you that you read most of it in your old boyfriend's bathtub.

And that, really, was the point of the library tour. It was an event put on by book people for book people — something we need more of at a time when non-book people seem increasingly eager to tell us we are fusty and impractical and obsolete. I came away from the library tour feeling that it was a signal flare set off to ask the question, "Are you out there?" And we showed up — crowds of us — and said, "Yes, we are.'

By Permission from Joan Wickersham

Joan Wickersham's column appears regularly in the *Boston Globe*. Her website is www.joanwickersham.com.

Ellsworth, KS Library – R. Pendleton

Your library is your portrait.

Holbrook Jackson

CHAPTER 5 – **CAKE PANS**

Our genealogy travels in 2001 took us first to South Dakota and then to Kansas. The following report is largely taken from the logs we made at that time.

Sometimes the towns are so small that there is only

one street. If you get to the cafe much after, say, noon, the Special is all gone and only sandwiches are available. When a combine moves through the wheat, clouds of chaff blow out behind and the kernels shoot up to a bin behind the driver. Trailer trucks full of wheat are parked at the elevators.

Everybody waves to everybody on the dirt roads, but not necessarily on the state highway. The major store is the hardware and feed store. And there is always some combination of town offices. But there is, almost always, a library.

In downtown Aberdeen, South Dakota, the office of the Register of Deeds holds photocopies of grant deeds, tax deeds, plats, probate records, all neatly bound in big binders. The clerk showed us where things were and left us to work on our own. Imagine doing that in your town! Pretty soon we were finding records of land transfers dating back to the days of the Dakota Territory. With the aid of the plots we found out where the relatives lived and worked and were buried.

After a hot dog and milkshake for lunch we drove to Groton, South Dakota (pop. 1000) where we got even more help. The tiny Wage Library doubled as the City Hall of Records, in the same building as all the city government and police. The library conveniently had an alphabetical file of obituaries clipped from the paper and a cemetery record list! We got two more obituaries and then headed to the offices of the *Groton Independent*, a weekly newspaper dating back to 1893.

The *Groton Independent* offices turned out to be a gift and floral shop, doubling as a newspaper office. A little Sheltie dog ran around checking us out. So we learned how tiny towns survive: by combining lots of part-time activities. The proprietess was just as helpful as the library / city hall staff, finding us a table to work and handing us ancient, cardboard bound files of browned and brittle nineteenth-century papers, full of news. John Wanamaker was purchasing land in Philadelphia; a young woman won her breach of promise suit against a congressman and had a nervous collapse right there in court (in Washington, D.C.); Coxey's army was protesting the lack of support for the unemployed veterans; lots of bargains could be bought for nineteen cents each.

Then we found Aaron Bell's obituary. It turned out Aaron and his wife Jane had moved to Dakota territory in 1887, to be near their son John, who had pioneered three years earlier. We made an extra photocopy for the library's obituary file. Forty-seven cents for the photocopies seemed like too little, so we managed to leave a little more, in hopes that the proprietess would still be in business for the next genealogy buff that comes to town.

Ellsworth and Wilson, Kansas, each have a town library, and the Ellsworth Public Library has a couple of microfilm readers and reels of newspapers from over a hundred years ago.

We spent a couple of days hunched over microfilm readers, reading old marriage records and obituaries. We found two great uncles who briefly owned a department store in Wilson and paid to have long flowery biographies placed in a book entitled Biographical History of Central Kansas. But for the most part, these people went to high school, then got married, farmed the land, raised cattle and families, and went to church.

The *Ellsworth Reporter* for June 8, 1922 told of an old sick bachelor who committed suicide and the accidental drowning, in a flash flood, of a nine-year-old; his older sister was able to save two siblings (including Elsa's grandfather).

We read quite a bit of other news and gossip, too, all jumbled together. The big social organizations here were the Odd Fellows and the Knights of Pythias. A hundred years ago there were racist stories; fifteen years after that we were fighting the Huns. And the paper was unabashedly Republican.

One of the libraries has a few bookshelves filled with cake pans of various unusual shapes. One can borrow these, just like books. The children like to pick out the shape of cake pan to have for their birthday parties.

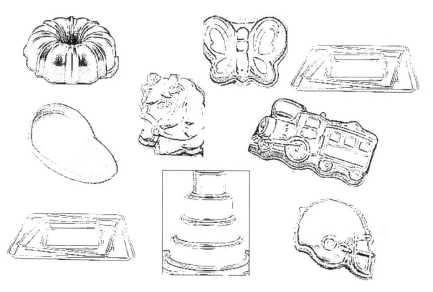

Cake Pans in Library – R. Pendleton

Korea U.S Army Bookmobile – A. Pastorius

The librarian must be the librarian militant before he can be the librarian triumphant.

Melvil Dewey

CHAPTER 6 - **BOOKMOBILE**

The bookmobile was a converted Ford package delivery truck that served the men of the 7th Infantry Division in Korea. The walls were lined with bookshelves. There was a small check out area in the front, a Pay system, turntable, and probably the only air conditioner in the country. The gear shift handle was an 8 ball undoubtedly stolen from a day room pool set. The lug nuts disappeared years before I rode on the bookmobile as had the brakes. The brakes were a hodgepodge of copper tubes and other parts manufactured by and found by GI and black market mechanics who worked on the vehicle.

As the Acting Area Librarian (acting because I was not eligible for the grade level) was to keep this mechanical monster operational. I who have a difficult time opening a Swiss Army knife without cutting myself. I pretended to know what I was doing by climbing down into the grease pit in the motor pool and sagely nodding my head while the mechanics explained the latest problem to me. The psychology which I learned from my predecessors was that if I looked like I knew what I was doing, maybe, just maybe the mechanics would try to repair the vehicle.

Civilian Army employees couldn't get driver's licenses in Korea during this time frame, the late 1960s, so the bookmobile was driven by Korean drivers with the library staff riding shot gun. A typical exchange went like this:

> Librarian, "Oh my God, watch out."
> Driver, "I driver, you no driver."
> Librarian, "I back seat driver. Old American custom."
> Driver, "You no in back seat. You in front seat."

Who could argue with that logic?

A tradition in which I never participated was to hold

an annual librarian drive, the purpose of which was to demonstrate that the librarians actually did know how to drive. After that the librarians who participated earned the right to say "Oh my God" a few times.

Mr. Pak was the lead driver. Tall and slim, with chiseled features, and a constant smile he was a delight to be around...except when someone messed with his bookmobile. Then he could be a Mamma Grizzly. In addition to being very amiable and responsible he had a photographic memory. This could be a good thing, and sometimes it could be a bad thing. There were 36 weekly stops, but Mr. Pak knew who had every book that was checked out, and the preferences of the men who constantly used the bookmobile. Mr. Pak was the first person to attack the shipments of new books. He would say, Sp4 Thompson likes Louis Lamour books, or Pvt. So and So requested this book." Frequently a soldier would try to check out a book, and Mr. Pak would say "you already read that." And sure enough the soldier's name would be on the book card record.

Unfortunately Mr. Pak saw no need to keep records, since he knew where everything was. When the bookmobile was side lined which happened frequently, books would be scattered through out the Division with no way for the rest of us to know where they were.

My run was Wednesday, the day we went to Line Papa. Line Papa was an area where the men of the Division were living out in the field building concrete bunkers. They lived in tents for months at a time and had no recreation except for occasional visits from the "Doughnut Dollies", i.e., Red Cross recreation staff.

Line Papa was so far away that we had to leave Camp Casey by 7:00 a.m. in order to return before dark. This was problematic when North Korean infiltrators were known to be in the area.

We had to take an armed guard with us. This necessitated lining up a guard with a rifle. No problem. The problem was that sometimes no one could find a key to the Arms Room before 9:00 a.m. Since the guards usually slung the rifles across their legs and fell asleep in the back of the truck we were probably safer with no ammunition. We never came across infiltrators but subsequently a tunnel was discovered that had its exit inside one of the tunnels we drove through on a regular basis.

I don't know how far we traveled, since the odometer didn't work, and distances were measured in time, not miles, in 1968 Korea. The roads were unpaved mountainous ruts. We shared the roads with farmers pulling huge hand carts laden with supplies and crops.

Bicyclists peddled to market sometimes with baskets of kittens for sale dangling from the handle bars and unconscious pigs slung across the seats. The pigs were fed Mockley, the local rice wine, and tied to the bikes after they passed out.

Pig on back of bike – A. Pastorius

Occasionally the bookmobile drivers would slam on the brakes which was a sign that a slicky boy was trying to steal books out of the window in the back of the truck.

On the Line Papa run lunch was at the Engineering Battalion. They had the foresight to build a huge dining tent, with a wooden floor, with a view of the valley floor and mountains beyond. Better than that they also built latrines with walls a feature that did not exist at any of the other stops. Nor were there any trees along the roadsides. The farmers chopped them down to make charcoal, therefore the Engineer Battalion stop was pretty critical.

My second favorite stop was the residence of the baby goat mascot. Unfortunately it grew up to be a mean Billy Goat who butted the Commanding Officer in the rear. No more goat.

The librarians did all of this while wearing pantyhose and tight, tight skirts which were part of our uniforms designed by a male tailor during or shortly after World War II. Not exactly dancing backwards in high heels but close.

Despite the backbreaking ride, the extreme heat and cold, and dust, the Bookmobile was probably the most rewarding experience I ever had as a librarian. It was providing music, air conditioning on blistery hot and humid days, books, and above all some attention for the troops who deserved it and more.

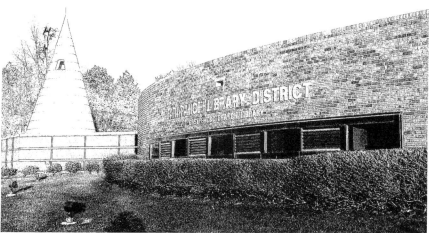
Castlewood, CO, Branch District Library – J. Bradley

A library is many things. It's a place to go, to get in out of the rain. It's a place to go if you want to sit and think. But particularly it is a place where books live, and where you can get in touch with other people, and other thoughts, through books.

E. B. White

CHAPTER 7 – **EVENING**

We are generally quiet at night because of the neighborhood, and tend to look forward to getting Caught Up. Especially me, because I'm working on trying to inject some hustle in my staff by switching jobs around, and it's just like with children -- you have to balance everything precisely or great howls of "unfair!" arise.

Anyway, we had just settled down, Maggie and me, when a giant knot of high school students swarmed in -- this only happens the night before a paper is due, naturally we are totally unprepared, this time it was "a book on a non-Christian Eastern religion I can read tonight and write a ten-page paper on before tomorrow morning." Of course!

While they were exploring the place, our Friends treasurer and her husband and toddler came in. They are the kind of people you always think are going to be very nice because they look nice -- very middle class and earnest and love to read. However. As usual, Mom had a terrible cold and snuffled and griped (she's also pregnant) and Father, in charge of the toddler while mom picked out books, encouraged the dreadful child to roam, and pluck the little cards out of the front of the card catalog drawers and pull on the scotch tape and remove the paperbacks from the rack to build a house with... and she is the Friends treasurer and the only one on the board who has done any work so far ... we gritted our teeth.

The place was filling up fast and so we at first did not notice the Lady Bum (we suspect she was the one who took her popcorn under the bushes and broke into the library, but not necessarily the one who shat in the stairwell -- did I tell you that story? A whole other tale). Anyway, this night she was nattily attired in little corduroy shorts and a see -through t-shirt, her incredible hair (it's black and phenomenally greasy, and she spends most of her in-library time sitting at a reading table playing with, braiding it and twisting it till you wonder why it simply doesn't let go and fall out) this time in a stiff greasy braid ticking straight up out of the middle of the top of her head. She installed herself at a reading table with the paper (all our bums know they have to read or get thrown out).

Next, Frank appeared to remind me that he was planning to have a showing of "Basta", a Chicano version of Scared Straight, for the Coalition to End Barrio Warfare ("no se olviden, mi barrio es tu barrio"). So he disappeared downstairs to monkey with the projector, and a steady stream of adolescent boys and girls, all Chicano, most tattooed, a lot of the boys wearing hairnets to train their hair into d.a.'s, came in the front door and wandered noisily downstairs.

The film was supposed to start at 7:00. At 8:00 they were still trying to get the projector to work. The kids (all of whom were total, scary strangers to me and in obvious dire need of being scared straight) began to wander upstairs again, for a drink of water, or a smoke, or just to kill time.

In the meantime, Maggie had come to me in distress to report that the Lady Bum had a bottle of wine on the table with her. I went to see. Sure enough, it was a bottle, the size and shape of a Ripple bottle but, incredibly, bearing the label of Jack Daniels. If it was Jack Daniels I'll eat my hat. I think it was -- well who knows what -- Ripple probably. Anyway, I mentioned that all food must be taken outside (!) and she answered amiably that she usually kept it in her purse but had taken it out to get at her mirror to look at her hair. We compromised on her putting it back in the purse.

The high school students were in the back of the library, trying to figure out a strategy for getting past the young gangsters without losing face. They eventually all moved out, fast, in a group, just like that carton of people getting off the subway at rush hour and walking along the street in a clump.

The Lady bum, having discovered the gangsters at the front door, decided it was time she had a smoke and a drink of water. The front porch smoke apparently not attracting enough attention, she went to the drinking fountain just inside, and stood there for a full seven minutes, drinking water, her little bum bum (sorry) sticking out in the aisle. Oh my the boys were distressed. Turns out they all needed a drink of water and she was taking it all. They asked her to give them a turn. She ignored them. They spoke loudly to each other about people who are impolite and hog the drinking fountain.

Just then one of our most proper intellectual ladies made a rare visit, inquiring courteously if these "children are often here in the evening". Unfortunately, I didn't stop to think and just said, "no you just got lucky" and she was not amused.

Frank and his team were still trying to make the projector work.

The boys wandered downstairs again, several with lit cigarettes in their hands. I managed to get to Frank and suggest, in my most non-judgmental manner, that he might like to talk to them about not smoking (he evidently did, because this morning there are 6 or 7 holes where cigarettes were stubbed out on the rug...)

So up they came and down they went, the lady bum paced back and forth, and I was glad to see a nice normal fat farmer-looking family come in. Mom, dad, and two kids, all round and rosy. They set right to work picking books and, distracted by the other things, I forgot them until about 8:20 (we close at 8:30) when we began to go around warning people and picking up. The lady bum left, and then I realized that the table in front of the farm family was completely covered with books.

You may remember that a) Kern County's philosophy is not to limit the number of books one may check out and b) to check out a book you have to write the author's last name, the title of the book, the copy number, and your name and address on a special slip. (That was the process at that time.)

Even with five books to a slip, it was going to be a long process, since only the mother was writing. In fact, as she sat and wrote, the rest of the family kept bringing her more books.

Well, closing time came and closing time went. We each individually had checked all possible lady-bum hiding places and were pretty sure she was out waiting to get to the bushes. But the farm mother wrote and wrote and wrote.

I have to admit that I was finally reduced to grabbing a book out of her hands (she pulled back and I pulled and won) and telling her that that was all. I was going home and so was she and that was that. She gave me a puzzled look and said "but I only wanted to fill up the slip" as though I should be remorseful. I was mainly hungry.

At that, Maggie and I thrust the family out the door and fled, leaving Frank, the cigarettes, the movie and 30 young toughs in the basement, where the projector was finally working like a charm.

The only problem is, that he has promised to repeat the film again tomorrow night. I think I am getting a sore throat.

Cleveland, OH Public Library Stokes Wing – R. Pendleton

*I can't write without a reader. It's precisely like a kiss—
you can't do it alone.*

John Cheever

CHAPTER 8 – **READERS AND WRITERS TEA**

The tall, shy, fourteen-year-old boy cleared his throat and began to read his poem. In the audience, the white-haired retired schoolteacher who would be next to read leaned forward, nodding encouragingly. From my post at the side of the make-shift podium I could see what the boy could see — adults and young people listening attentively to his tale of unicorns and fair maidens. I began to relax; the first-ever Friends of the Library Readers and Writers Tea was a rousing success.

Our town is a small, isolated town in the Mojave Desert. Until World War II, most residents were prospectors or land speculators hoping (until the Los Angeles aqueduct was built) to plant orchards in irrigated desert soil. The war brought the United States Navy: military and civilian rocket scientists needed the vast empty lands of the dry lakebed and clear skies for aircraft and weapons testing.

Over the next half-century, many scientists and engineers, mechanics and pilots, store-keepers and teachers turned temporary military duty into a life-time career, remaining in the high desert even when they retired. Our isolation provided strong motivation for clubs and activities of all kinds, from bicycle races to photography to astronomy (those clear skies with no city lights!). Lately, as the Navy budget decreases, jobs disappear and the population ages, many of the traditional groups have dwindled to a half-dozen or so hardy members.

The Friends of the Library found itself in this predicament last summer. Although our membership list contains more than a hundred names, our meetings can be held around one library table, and generally consist of the usual mind-numbing committee reports.

However, we recently acquired a peppy and peppery octogenarian as our Treasurer. At each meeting he would express, in vigorous terms, his displeasure that all of our meetings were business meetings. Where was the fun? He would ask. Where are the programs? There were plenty of interesting people in town; why didn't we invite somebody to come and talk to us?

One evening, he followed his speech with a definite offer: if we provided a program, he would make the cookies. And he would even bring the punch bowl. As president (and equally bored with committee reports), I supported the idea, and found myself rhapsodizing on Gracious Living.

"Lace tablecloths," I said. "Little sandwiches with the crusts cut off! Flowers on the serving table."

The others began to stir. We decided we wanted mints in a china dish and real tea. We needed little tarts with one strawberry pressed into the whipped cream, or maybe scones.

You could almost feel a buried ancestral memory of college Sunday dinners, high teas, and luncheons with Grandmamma. This is a town where dressing up means wearing a shirt with buttons, and "desert casual" is an accepted term on invitations. A lace-tablecloth Tea would be uncommon, to say the least.

But what kind of program would we have? Certainly we couldn't afford to pay to hire an author (and spending our money that way, when we couldn't afford to give the library a subscription to the *New York Times*, would have caused mutiny). We left that little detail till the next meeting and went home to practice making cucumber sandwiches.

Sometime before the next meeting, the inspiration hit. We would invite local authors and readers to share their talents. It was as though we had jumped back in time to the early days at the Navy base, when you might put together a chamber music evening, or check out a play script from the library to read aloud, or gather friends to produce a pun-filled, goofy play you'd written.

At the next Friends' meeting, enthusiasm was almost palpable, even though it was the same small group. We quickly agreed on the ground rules:

Anybody who wants to read something can participate.

You must sign up in advance (so that your name can appear on the program and so that we can plan when to have the intermission).

Your selection should be no longer than five minutes (in case it is truly terrible. Anybody can stand five minutes of awful prose or poetry).

And that was it. No auditions, no advance editorial judgments. We made flyers and posted them in the library, and in the bookstore. We hoped that we'd have enough readers to fill an hour.

For the first time in years, Friends' officers and members met for lunch between meetings, and called each other, and made lists and generally got ready for the Tea. Additional flyers appeared on the supermarket bulletin board, in the bookstores, and on the library's circulation desk. There was, of course, some confusion. Several people called to make reservations just to be part of the audience (reservations! We'd never had a meeting with more than twenty-two people!). Some people wanted to read, but couldn't decide on a title (we correctly guessed that they hadn't exactly written the piece yet).

Finally we were ready to print the program, having selected a nice rippled parchment-looking set of computer printer paper, which would look handsome in a reader's scrapbook. To our surprise, we had a full slate of readers.

On the evening of the tea, the excitement was somewhat marred by the fact that the library's air conditioning had failed early in the morning (remember, this is August in the Mojave Desert). We sent our secretary out for extra ice for the punch because the first sack of ice had melted completely upon contact with the ginger ale. The library staff lent us big floor fans that we couldn't use because they drowned out the speakers. By the time we were ready to begin, each seat was filled and people were standing in the doorway.

Originally, I had resisted including an intermission, fearful that we would lose our audience, but the evening required frequent breaks for punch and ice water. Just about everybody stayed till the end, when they had the best, most unexpected treat of all: a selection of humorous verse from a retired schoolteacher.

Encouraged by the response to the original tea, we have held two additional programs. Our only change was to move to the art gallery in our local museum, which provides a bigger room and a public address system. On the evening of the second program, our town was rocked by a bigger-than-usual earthquake. Nevertheless, we had another full house.

The Friends of the Library have discovered a route to success, at least here. We have increased our membership, and we have certainly publicized the library in the community. But I believe the lessons we have learned are wider-ranging.

A. There are many, many talented and hard-working writers in our town. We have heard a semi-fictional account of one woman's family history; a mood picture of the desert at night; an astonishing variety of poetry, from lyrical, rhymed, and metered verse to an extended prose poem attacking the Los Angeles Department of Water and Power.

B. The quality of work was much higher than we had any right to expect. Of all of the four dozen or so selections, two at most were wearisome. None was offensive. All demonstrated that the writers had worked hard polishing their work.

C. Limiting the selections to five minutes each may be too rigorous (if you are not a speedy reader, you can only cover about 750 words in that time). The advantage, however, is a grand variety for an evening's entertainment.

D. Refreshments are an absolute necessity. They provide, in addition to sustenance (and prevention of dehydration out here) the opportunity to mix and chat, and the reminder that some serious cultural event is happening.

E. We never attempted to capture the readings in print. The readers took their manuscripts home with them at the end of the evening. The only memories are the program listings. The ephemeral nature of the evening seems to appeal to audience and reader alike.

F. The young readers gave a special charm and excitement to the programs. We heard some extraordinarily talented adolescents, for whom sharing their emotions with a group of strangers must have taken great courage. Their reward — sustained applause and appreciative comments from the audience — validated their efforts.

Our treasurer claims that repeat attendance is due to the excellence of his cookies, but something more mysterious and magical was also happening. We are familiar with recitals for amateur musicians, and craft and art shows for our local painters and potters, but the idea of a recital of prose and poetry is almost unknown. We had, without realizing it, re-established the ancient, universal tradition of sharing gifts. We had produced a rare event in which writers weren't required to compete with each other; each work was appreciated for its own merits.

The poets knew best how their work would sound aloud, but the story-readers and the essayists seemed, each time, to experience a moment of surprise as they heard their words spoken. Most readers read their own work, and most read well. Several members of the audience commented that "maybe next time" they will, also, be ready to present their work.

And by the end of each evening, as we packed up the few remaining cookies, we could hear in the many conversations the same gratifying phrase repeated over and over: "I didn't know you could write like that!" Writing almost always is either solitary or competitive; perhaps the Tea, repeated here and copied elsewhere, can provide an encouraging alternative.

Eugene Field Library (Denver, CO) – J. Bradley

A library is where you meet fascinating characters you never forget.

Judy Blume

CHAPTER 9 – **THE BLESSING**

Children's programs have an important place in libraries, and even small branches often have someone, to manage them. I was fortunate in that my first position out of library school was such a job.

Armed with my MLIS and my own experience as a mother and as a child who loved to read, I began my career.

Some of my responsibilities were already established. I was to develop preschool story times and the summer reading program, and visit schools to publicize library programs and promote reading. The branch supervisor and county head of children's services also encouraged me to develop other children's programs that could be tied into books and reading. I took that as a personal challenge and worked on several programs. Some were complete disasters, and we all agreed to never repeat them. One of those was the Cinco de Mayo celebration, complete with a piñata free-for-all which endangered the life of everybody in the room – truly scary. The other was our Pet Show/Animal Blessing.

The idea for the animal blessing came from memories of the annual blessing in the city of Los Angeles held at the Mission downtown near Olvera Street. There was always a lot of press coverage and it seemed like a fun time for all. Although the Archbishop usually handled the blessing, it didn't seem like a religious event as much as it was a community celebration for children and their pets. I saw this as a great opportunity to promote favorite children's books for all ages. For preschoolers there was *Make Way for*

Ducklings, The Runaway Bunny, Curious George, and so many other beautiful picture books. Older readers could be enticed by books about various types of animals, and how to care for their pets. I would also display some of the classics: *Charlotte's Web, Mr. Popper's Penguins*, and *Stuart Little.* Older children and young adults would see copies of *Where the Red Fern Grows, The Yearling, Lad, a Dog* and *Black Beauty*.

Of course there were many details to work out. After outlining the plan and logistics we received permission to use our meeting room. We thought since all our programs before had been held there, and the room could accommodate up to 80, we would have no problems. But who would bless the animals? We felt it needed to be someone who had the authority and ability to do so. Father Clooney, the Catholic priest, would be ideal, but would he agree? It could sound very frivolous, and we had never heard of it happening in town before. Would he insist upon it being at the church? The only way to find out was to call him, so I did.

I was really intimidated by the thought of a conversation. Father Clooney, soon to be Monsignor Clooney, was a well-loved Irish priest who had been in town for years. He had a delightful brogue and a human touch that endeared him to his parishioners and allowed him to minister to his congregation with charm and grace. He treated everyone with respect and was seen as a major figure in the community. I had never met him personally and was not a member of his church so calling him was not easy. I wondered if he would even talk to me. I found him easy to talk to, and he treated my request with a careful dignity that I appreciated. He agreed to hold a blessing and was willing to come to the library for it. I was thrilled and immediately became a big fan.

We decided to hold the event during Spring break when the students were out of school and in need of activities. We sent out articles to both local papers, the local radio stations, and had flyers and information in the library. We stipulated that all animals needed to be on leashes or in cages for their own protection as well as the children's. We planned on awarding prizes for largest, smallest, furriest, etc., consisting of certificates and free ice cream cone coupons from the local stores. The stores were kind enough to give them to us, since we had no budget for such events.

Finally the day arrived and the animals and their owners began to show up. We had anticipated the usual dogs and cats and birds, but were totally unprepared for the horse. One horrified look from the janitor and I decided he had to wait outside the meeting room in the grass, but we kept the door open so the owner could still participate. In addition to the large, medium, and small dogs and cats, we had rabbits and tortoises, a rat, ducks, parakeets and a cockatiel. We did our best to keep order, but soon there were too many animals and too much going on. We may have forgotten that cats want to kill rats and birds, but the cats remembered. Apparently some females were in heat, and the male dogs of all sizes knew that.

The worst was one little pit bull that was ready to tear up every other dog in the room. I finally had to ask his owner to take him outside too, despite her saying that he had never behaved like that before, and that he was not dangerous.

As we waited for Father Clooney, it was obvious that keeping them all cooped up in the room was a recipe for disaster. So, we held an impromptu parade.

We lined up the animals and the owners and began a slow walk around the block, praying that Father Clooney would please show up so we could send them all home before something happened. We passed the court, the Post Office and the Police and the Fire Stations, attracting all kinds of attention with the animals in cages, on shoulders, with leashes and the horse at the end. Fortunately by the time we came back to the front of the library Father Clooney had arrived, and he was wonderful.

Adorned in beautiful white robes with gold trim and carrying a censor that gave off appropriate puffs of smoke, he began his rites. He spoke in Latin, and walked among the animals and their owners on the lawn in front of the library. The press arrived and got some wonderful pictures of him touching the heads of animals and children and praying over them. We were all impressed. It took less than 15 minutes of his time, but he seemed to enjoy it and treated it with humor and dignity. It was a great success. I loved Father Clooney!

When he left, we quickly gave out our certificates and told everyone that the blessing was complete. I didn't even try to give any book talks or promote summer reading. I knew the staff and the groundskeepers and janitors wanted the animals gone before any more of them decided to mark their territory or worse. Seeing the departure of that pit bull was the biggest relief ever. Checking out the meeting room later, I was glad not to find any remains outside of a few feathers.

We held a meeting to discuss what we had learned. Although we all agreed that everyone had a wonderful time, and it was great publicity, we were very lucky. We didn't have any attacks – primarily because the pit bull's owner was good with the leash, but what a possibility for disaster, not to mention a huge lawsuit!

We also heard from the janitor and the groundskeepers that they did not want a repeat, and we had to agree.

Once was enough!

Chicago, IL Storefront Library – R. Pendleton

NO ANIMALS ALLOWED

Unnamed library rule

CHAPTER 10 - **CRITTERS**

Some libraries are home to various pets, and may sponsor special animals for a variety of reasons. Programs with service dogs and guide dogs in training are one popular way for the library to provide community service. Humane societies may sponsor information or adoption programs and help instruct in pet care. Programs on endangered species and wildlife may offer information and exhibits of alligators, desert tortoises, owls, snakes, monkeys, etc. These programs often provide a tie-in to a story time or reading program. Animals bring people to the library to enjoy the experience and a chance to interact.

Some animals even live in libraries. Cats are a particular favorite and some have become famous. The most well-known is probably Dewey, the Library Cat who was rescued from a book drop one wintry night and lived in the Spencer, Iowa, public library. His story was captured in *Dewey, the Library Cat: a True Story*, by the librarian, Vickie Myron. During the mid-1980's, the public library in Minden, Nevada, named its library cats Baker and Taylor after the well-known book distributor. The Scottish Fold cats soon became the company's official mascots, with their distinctive folded-ear heads decorating posters, bags, and other memorabilia.

Worldwide, there are estimated to be hundreds of library cats. They have been found in almost every State and in many foreign countries. Although some are installed as mousers, many are pets who provide companionship or become the unofficial greeters of the library. Some library cats, perhaps out of fear of allergy attacks, are merely virtual, some are statues and a few have even been stuffed. A Maine Coon cat named Diesel stars in the *Cat in the Stacks* Mystery series with his librarian owner, Charlie. Royal Reggie, a library cat, inspired a Library Cat Society. Wesleyan College in Georgia has an informative web page featuring Libris, their official library cat.

Cats and other library mascots do come with some issues. Cats and other animal allergies are the most common problems, but bites or attacks are the worst; one rarely hears of a library dog. Many libraries have had to banish their cats for "cause." L.C. was a library cat at the public library in Escondido, California, until the city was sued. L.C. reportedly attacked an assistance dog. The city wisely retired him while trying to resolve a large claim. Although the claim was dismissed as frivolous, L.C. was never allowed to return to the library. He reportedly lived out his retired life quite comfortably in a private home.

As an animal lover and owner, and a children's librarian, I thought it would be fun to "liven" up the children's area in our public library. I really wanted a library cat, so I tossed around the idea of furred creatures to the rest of the staff, but concern for sanitation, allergies, bites and care caused them to be vetoed. We arrived at a compromise where a small creature, properly caged, without teeth and not known to cause allergy or disease might be permitted, although it would have to be housed in such a way that it could not escape, nor could it be easily removed by a library visitor. We knew children would want to play with the creature, but we couldn't allow that for so many reasons.

At that point it seemed my options were limited. I knew from my personal experience how easy it was for mice, rats, rabbits, and guinea pigs to escape, and I knew many adults would call for an immediate expulsion of a lizard or snake of any type. I began to think nothing would work. But a visit to the pet shop convinced me otherwise. A small turtle was available with a nice glass aquarium complete with locking top (this was before the connection between turtles and salmonella was widely known).

The turtle was a red-eared pond slider, a bigger version of the one we all used to get from the dime store or won as a prize when the carnival came to town. The turtles then were tiny adorable things brightly painted with nail polish and decorated with flower decals. They never lived long and were doomed when they were painted or given to children who had no idea how to care for them. This larger version evoked nostalgia and I was easily talked into buying him. The pet shop clerk instructed me in his proper care, informing me that the only food to keep him healthy was live goldfish. By this point I was too committed to change my mind, so home he came.

The next day, Ringo, named by a Beatles fan, appeared in a sunny spot in the library with a card chock full of turtle information. He was very popular from the beginning and many children enjoyed visiting him. I thought he was a nice addition to the library and willingly took on his care and feeding. The care consisted of cleaning his habitat on a regular basis and feeding him in the evenings after we closed. The feeding of the live goldfish was too much for some of the staff, who preferred not to know the gory details. I did have to keep live goldfish on hand in the back room, though we thought it best the children did not see or know- the details of Ringo's diet.

Things went well and Ringo grew and grew. He soon outgrew his small aquarium and was moved to a larger one. That was a problem to move and clean but I persevered. The live goldfish at the pet store were soon replaced by frozen goldfish that we had to keep in the staff refrigerator freezer. Some of the staff were not appreciative. Since I was not there every evening and Ringo needed to eat often, some of the other staff had to volunteer to help with the feeding. There was a bit of grumbling, but Ringo had many friends and the staff rallied to see that he was well fed and healthy.

As Ringo grew from eight to nine inches to beyond, he had to be moved to a larger home. At this point, no one could actually lift the aquarium, even with only a small amount of water in it. To clean the habitat we had to remove Ringo and the rocks and carefully empty the water. The water, which was full of turtle scat and dead goldfish pieces, was quite disgusting and we could easily imagine getting ill from the contact. The staff grumbling grew louder and louder.

My initial investment had grown over time, especially as his diet grew. Goldfish became more expensive and larger aquariums cost even more. Ringo looked less like a child's pet and more like a predator as he grew in size and attitude.

During the Ringo era, we had a desert tortoise program each year. They were very popular since we had many tortoises show up in our town or on the highway each Spring. The leading tortoise expert visited Ringo each year and commented on his health and environment. His comments became less favorable as he saw Ringo outgrow his tank, and he became concerned that Ringo needed a larger area. Although I agreed, I wasn't sure how to resolve it. As Ringo needed more room, so did the children's book collection. There was no good place for a larger aquarium.

The staff breathed a sigh of relief when I decided that we should move Ringo out of the library. With our desert tortoise connection we found an amphibian fancier who knew how to care for turtles as well as tortoises and was willing to take on Ringo. It was a bittersweet ending. A few of the patrons missed Ringo but they all understood why he needed to leave. The staff was happier not to have to care for him, and I wasn't sure how I felt.

I still longed for a library cat. But that was not to be.

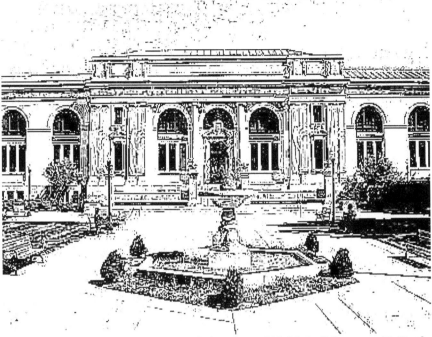

Columbus OH, Main Library – D. Butler

Books to the ceiling,
Books to the sky,
My pile of books is a mile high.
How I love them! How I need them!
I'll have a long beard by the time I read them.

Arnold Lobel

CHAPTER 11 – **COCKROACH MAN**

Public libraries have regulars, patrons that come
every week or two, usually on the same day and time.
Over time, the staff becomes acquainted with them

and often friendly as their reading interests may connect with their own. Staff checking out books might be heard to say, "Oh, you'll like that one," or "She's written a new one we just received, would you like it too?"

Most library users are in a good mood and communicating is easy. Staff members know not to be nosy if someone is checking out *How To Do Your Own Divorce* or *What To Expect During Your Pregnancy*, even when they can't help but notice. The people who don't communicate with staff are respectfully helped to check out books and use the computers, or find materials on requested topics. Even the youngest users are given the courtesy that is their due.

That doesn't mean that some users aren't grouchy or difficult. It isn't just the homeless or the mentally ill that can be a challenge; the regulars can also try one's patience.

One such, was an older gentleman, Mr. C, who came every other Tuesday evening at approximately 7:30, apparently after he finished his dinner. Staff could usually tell because he often had remainders of his dinner on his clothing, a small spot or stain or string of food. He also usually smelled like the garlic or onions that he must have eaten at every meal. Between his smells and semi-dirty appearance he was not fun to be near.

Still, he was given the same respect and help that all patrons received, and despite all that, he was usually short with staff, grouchy, and disagreeable. Now, we can look back and assume he may have been ill or lonely, or depressed. Then, we knew we just didn't want to help him with his books if at all possible. It wasn't just his smell or his attitude that made us avoid him, it was the books he returned. They too seemed dirty and faintly aromatic of his dinner.

He always came in carrying a large brown paper grocery bag full of books. He would empty the bag into the book slot at the circulation desk, adding dirt and grime to the piles of books already waiting there. If we saw him in time, we quickly pulled out the books already in the slot, so that they wouldn't have dirt on them too but we couldn't always see him in time, and there were often small piles of dirt or grit that had to cleaned out later. Yuck.

In any public place, you expect to encounter dirt and germs, but this was getting to be annoying. We wondered why he didn't use a clean bag, or why after emptying the contents each time, there was still dirt in the bag for the next time. We knew the books we checked out didn't have dirt on them; that just didn't happen in the library. The janitor was careful about cleanliness, and his supervisor regularly checked to make sure that he was. Library volunteers washed the covers of all books that came in needing that, including all of Mr. C's books.

The regular Tuesday night staff was Cheryl and Mamie. Both were women with clean houses who enjoyed working in a clean environment. Mr. C's dirty books didn't sit well with them. They talked about it, and decided they would intercept Mr. C. and take the bag while it still contained the dirty books and empty the bag into the trash cans in the back room where Mr. C couldn't see what they did. That way, there would be no dirt in the book slot and no more mess to clean up.

Tuesday night came, and Mr. C. walked in. carrying his usual brown bag. Cheryl saw him first and reached for the bag. "We're looking for a special book and checking all the ones being returned," she said politely. He didn't seem ready to part with his bag. "We really need to find it," she said, "Could I please have your bag to check for the book?" she asked, reaching for the bag. "Well, I suppose," he said, but I want my bag back." "Fine" she said. "It will just take a second."

Cheryl carried the bag into the back room, and noticed up close, how very dirty and greasy the bag was. She hadn't noticed before, but then she had never seen it close before; Mr. C kept the bag with him. As she walked she noticed that it didn't smell very nice either. As she began to pull the books out of the bag so that she could dump the dirt she noticed something dark that was on top of one of the books. As she focused in on it, she saw that it was a large, very lively cockroach.

How she kept from screaming, she didn't know, but she dropped the bag into the trash. Gratefully, she noticed that the books were all out, and she didn't have to touch it again, especially when she saw another, smaller cockroach crawl out of the bag and make its way onto the floor. She stomped on the two cockroaches and tried to steady herself. It was just too gross for her. No one should have to do this; library workers shouldn't have to be exterminators too.

She found a clean new bag, and took it out to Mr. C. He looked at it and said, "This is not my bag, where is it?" Cheryl was so startled that she just blurted out, "It's in the back, but it was kind of dirty." He glared at her and said, "I want my bag." She knew she didn't want to touch the bag, but she was also sure it was empty of everything now. At a loss for another idea, she walked slowly into the back and gingerly picked up a corner of the bag with two fingers. She brought it back to Mr. C. The whole episode had really unsettled her. She couldn't think of what to say or do.

Later, as Mamie checked out the new books for Mr. C, Cheryl cringed as she saw him open up the bag and drop them in. After the library closed for the night, and Cheryl and Mamie and the others were leaving, Cheryl told them what had happened. They all were pretty disgusted and couldn't understand Mr. C's need for the same bag, when the one Cheryl had tried to give him was much better. Few people used bags to return their library books. The fabric recyclable bags were not yet very popular, and most people carried their books in their arms. He was just weird and he made them uncomfortable. He was big and not at all pleasant. Still, they wanted to get rid of that bag, and hoped to replace it.

The next day, they brought it up with the branch supervisor, who sympathized, but didn't really have a solution. "It's his bag, I suppose we can't really take it from him without his consent" she considered. Mamie seemed to be thinking about it, and finally told the others. "I think I can get rid of it. I'll try something next time." She didn't say any more, and the others didn't want to talk more about it, it was just too much.

Two weeks later, on Tuesday night, Mr. C showed up as he usually did, looking grumpy, dirty, and carrying the same bag! Cheryl glanced at Mamie to be sure she had seen him. She had, and she walked quickly toward the book slot from behind the desk as he approached from the front. As he held out the bag in order to tip his books into the slot, she quickly pulled it toward her. "Let me just help you with that," she said in her sweetest voice. She could be very sugary. He was so surprised that he didn't stop her. As she pulled the bag toward herself, one hand slipped and she grabbed the other corner of the bag, with just one hand and yanked up. The bag began to tear as the weight of the books pulled the side apart.

"Oh my, "she said, as the bag ripped all the way open, and she slid the books out. "I'm so sorry. I didn't realize how fragile your bag was. Please forgive me, I'll let you have one of our bags to replace yours." She and Cheryl were both happy to note there were no bugs in the bag this time. She smiled up at Mr. C with her most endearing smile. "I'll be right back, and you can choose whatever bag you want."

She soon returned with several brand new paper bags, which she offered, to Mr. C. "Please take one, and I promise to be more careful." Mr. C seemed to know that he had been fooled, but this sweet lady was always so kind and gentle, how could he be sure it was not an accident. The bag was old, and the books were heavy. He looked into her face, and she continued to smile in her sweet way. He snatched a bag and walked away. Cheryl turned away from the desk to keep from laughing. Mamie fooled people all the time with her quiet soft-spoken way. The staff knew what a steel magnolia she really was, and they admired her for her it.

The Tuesday nighters kept their eye on Mr. C and his bag. He seemed to have learned something from his encounter. He never returned the books in a dirty bag after that, although Cheryl was heard to comment, "Mamie, can you please do something about his breath too?"

Perth, NB Public Library - R. Pendleton

Librarian is a service occupation. Gas station attendant of the mind.

Richard Powers

CHAPTER 12 – **COCKROACH WOMAN**

I was hired to provide community library services at a time when library budgets were robust in the mid-1970s. One of my responsibilities was providing books to shut-ins who couldn't get to the library. It was challenging as I had to navigate through some tough neighborhoods. I often felt like I should have another person accompany me on these trips.

One very nice older woman needed our services, and was a voracious reader. She was disabled and home-bound. I filled two of the large tough canvas book bags for her every two weeks. Bringing them up to her house gave me pause, as it was really a small shack and the exterior was unkempt. I suspected she needed a lot more help than just the book deliveries. I always made my rounds in the daytime. The inside of her front door and living room looked okay on a quick first impression.

But, there turned out to be an issue that I had to address each time I picked up the bags full of return books and dropped off her new ones. That was the cockroaches. Yes, I delivered clean bags of books, but the bags I picked up were full of the yucky critters. I couldn't even take them inside the library building, but had to dump them on the loading dock first. I watched for a couple of minutes to make sure that all the roaches scurried out and then gingerly picked up the books and bags to bring into the library's back work area. I did not try to squish the roaches, live and let live outside of the building. Of course, we called the woman the cockroach lady.

Sadly for her, library budgets suffered after a state proposition passed. Library services lost funding, and jobs were lost. I was given a pink slip since community services like this were no longer included in our budget. The shut-in services were stopped, along with the books-by-mail program, and the library services to county jail inmates.

Luckily, another position opened up at a different county branch, and I was selected to fill it. I no longer traveled the mean streets, and no longer visited the cockroach lady. I wondered what happened to her, but was very happy not to be the bearer of cockroaches any longer.

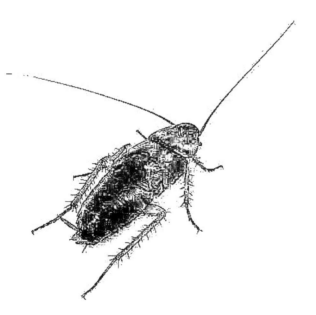

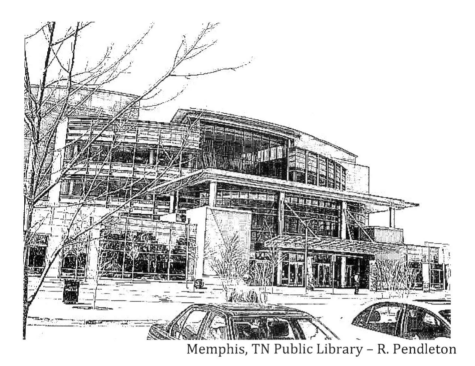

Memphis, TN Public Library – R. Pendleton

Reading to kids is to ordinary reading what jazz is to a string quartet.

Sean Wilentz

CHAPTER 13 – **STORY HOUR**

I had my first indication that this was going to be a challenging hour when the first two children showed up one hour early.

Courtney and Meghan are about 5 years old. Meghan's dad brings her to the library almost every day, in the afternoon, and almost every day she appears with a new Beanie Baby. Courtney is apparently Meghan's best friend. Courtney is ferociously intelligent with an intense interest in science, sharks in particular. She has just had a new baby brother about whom she refuses to speak. Courtney and Meghan look like twins but as far as I can tell they are not. Anyway, Dad and the two girls settled down to look at books while waiting.

Dad started reading to Meghan, with a continual accompaniment by Courtney who had found a shark book ("597. I know that number.") and was going on and on about cartilage and how shark teeth grow back if they get knocked out. (Dad, I should mention, is impossibly patient with the children).

I started off with *Zoo, Where are you?* C and M thought it was too babyish, the littles thought it was too long. One little boy called out "Excuse me! Excuse me! I would like to hear about volcanoes!"

Two of the children closest to the bookshelves helped themselves to a book each and began to study the pages. "I have one rule," I said pleasantly (?). "I read the books. Nobody else gets a book until after the stories." I collected the contraband books.

I had decided to read parade stories because that's what I found on the shelves. I'll admit it was a mistake including *Make Way For Ducklings* — boy, is that book long — but they actually kind of liked it, especially since I roared out the names of the ducklings, and encouraged them to quack along.

During the next book some of them who hadn't quite got the concept were still quacking. "Excuse me! Excuse me!" It was volcano boy, of course. "That girl is quacking." I ignored him.

Somewhere soon I started *Madeline*. EVERYBODY knows *Madeline*, so there was a little chorus from time to time, especially about Miss Clavell — "Something is not Well!"

As I finished each book, I stood it up on the floor, intending that the children could choose them to borrow at the conclusion of the story hour. When I moved on to the next story, Selena picked up *Madeline* and began to read it aloud to herself, in a language which was not demonstrably English but which seemed to explain the pictures. She kept right on with *Madeline*, in a small soprano, throughout the rest of the hour. Another girl picked up *Make Way For Ducklings*.

You'd think the time was almost up, but it was only about 20 minutes into the hour.

"Excuse me! Excuse me!" Little snot. "That girl took a book. She is not supposed to take a book. That is a rule!" Little fascist.

I stared at the little girl. "I read, you sit." She plopped down on the floor, dropping the book. Two great tears formed and began to slide down her cheeks. I was unmoved.

We had two more parade books, both short, both rather dumb. Then I got everybody formed up for The

Best Part. We paraded all through the library clapping our hands. The idea was to vary the activity, since I can't remember any finger plays except for the *Itsy-Bitsy Spider.* I'm saving it for a Truly Desperate Occasion. So there we go, me at the head, twelve little clapping ducklings enthusiastically following along, marching through the library.

"Excuse me! We should stamp our feet!" Actually, not a bad idea. So we did.

As I passed one of the moms, she murmured, bemused, "I thought we should be quiet in the library!" She's a home schooler. and I probably undid months of serious work on her part. But I like loud libraries, myself.

When we got back, they were ready for more stories. Except for Selena, who had carried *Madeline* through the parade and was at the part where the girls visit her in the hospital.

Meghan had brought two of her beanie babies which she insisted on sharing (passing them around so everybody could pat them). This was because during the Christmas stories I'd had my granddaughter Emily's *Stellaluna* bat and had passed it around. The children were rigorous about making sure that everybody had the same number of pats of the Beanie Babies. In retrospect, I find that rather chilling.

I had promised a dog story, so I read a Rosemary Wells *McDuff* book. That took care of making Meghan's doggie Beanie Baby relevant.

I think I have forgotten the two or three stories I finished with — I was gradually losing my audience as mothers swept in and removed wriggly, tired, and cranky children, one by one. Selena fell asleep holding *Madeline*.

The story hour didn't really end — it collapsed.

Brenda says "it went as well as you could expect, considering."

San Luis Obispo, CA Library – J. Bradley

When I got my library card, that's when my life began.

Rita Mae Brown

CHAPTER 14 – **THE BOOK**

My older sister and I were in ninth and tenth grade when *Peyton Place* was first published. My mother had never initiated censorship in our reading and we were among the first of our group to understand the "facts of life." But we didn't know how she would feel about the book with its scandalous sex. So when we bought a paperback copy from a newsstand we didn't tell her. We liked the book and bought *Return to Peyton Place* when it came out too. When we found our mother reading her own copy of *Peyton Place* we confessed that we had the sequel and she asked to borrow it when we were done. We all agreed it was not great literature, but fun to read. We laughed about it at the time, and it paid off, because when I was reading more adult titles in the eleventh and twelfth grade some had the "adult only" red stripe on them, and my mother could assure the librarian in our small branch library that she approved of my reading those books.

The issue of a request to remove or ban a book is so often raised that most libraries have a standard process to deal with it, and forms to complete to initiate that. To be prepared, libraries have also wisely made public their selection criteria for purchasing books and other materials. The issue is often based on sexual or religious content and usually is raised if parents or teachers believe that youth should be protected from such material. The process begins when a parent registers a verbal complaint. We ask if the person initiating the complaint had read the entire book, since many passages are problematic taken out of context but wouldn't upset the reader if the entire book was read. Often they had not read the entire book; once they had read it they would not follow through with the request.

Today the issue is often enmeshed with technology. As libraries become centers for the public use of computers, the censorship issue is often raised with the decision to install filtering software on the computers, or whether to permit children to use computers – they might stumble onto the "wrong sites." Without filtering software, the public is often exposed to the odd individual who uses the public computer for his not so private pornographic journeys through cyberspace.

The story I relate is from a simpler time, when computers were not part of the daily life, and the library had only books and a few videos. I was the children's librarian of a medium-sized public library, and I had already had a few experiences with censorship. I had dealt with parents whose concerns led them to initiate a protest against a book. I was feeling pretty confident about my ability to handle these attempts to remove books because all of the parents who were given the forms to complete failed to return them, and the protests died before they began. The forms were not complicated or difficult to complete, but it often gave the complainer time to reflect upon the book and change his or her mind.

I was used to individuals who felt that some of the material in the "hygiene" (the words sex education were never spoken) books was too explicit for their child. They often agreed that the more unfortunate child whose parent or clergy did not provide enough guidance might actually need the information in the book. Often they found an adult book that their child had brought home which we could show was intended for adults. They then understood that they had the ability to shield their child themselves if they accompanied him to the library to select books they felt were appropriate.

Having deflected many complaints, I was feeling pretty confident until a patron brought up a picture book and told me that it was dangerous for children to have it on our shelves. I asked the patron the usual questions, and she had read the entire book, as she had read it to her four-year-old. She did not take the book out of context and was sure it was going to cause harm some time. I gave her the usual forms to complete and hoped we had heard the last of it. I was wrong.

She returned with the forms the following week and brought the book to me at the desk, requesting that I remove it from the shelf. I took the book from her and kept it off the shelf pending our inquiry into her request to remove it. I admit I was puzzled by the entire thing but felt some responsibility because I was the children's librarian and I was supposed to know the collection. I had read this book, which was pure fantasy, and I didn't see that it would endanger a child.

The book was titled *The Steamroller: a Fantasy*. It was written by a noted children's author, Margaret Wise Brown, and illustrated by Evaline Ness, another well-known children's book favorite. In the story, a young girl, Nancy, mysteriously receives a single Christmas gift – the steamroller. She takes the gift out for a ride and flattens many things along the way, one of which was human, as I recall. I believe the human popped back up, unrealistically. The complaint was that it was too violent and that a child might believe it was possible to flatten someone without any lasting consequence. It was really intended for a child older than four, but since it was a picture book, it could easily be picked up and read by a preschooler.

I had mixed feelings about the book. It was not a classic like *Goodnight Moon*, the author's most famous contribution to children's literature, nor did it have a great message that all children would benefit from hearing multiple times. It was fantastic and pretty macabre if you looked at it that way. I had never seen a parent say how wonderful *The Steamroller* was or have a child laugh delightedly while reading it. I could see the parent's point of view, but I frankly disagreed with her assessment that it was dangerous. But what was the principle here? What right was I trying to protect?

I was feeling guilty because I had erred in the past with an event where this same woman and her child were in attendance. It was a Halloween themed story time, and I had shown a children's cartoon video that had a scary witch in it. The witch was not scary in the book version, but the film version did frighten some of the younger children. We turned it off and went to a less scary book, but I felt bad that I had not previewed the film first, because I was familiar with the book. I should have known better but it did occur and I remembered the woman was justifiably not happy.

I was truly confused, so I asked others. I spoke to the branch supervisor and to the county head of children's services. Neither of them had strong feelings about the book, but neither felt that a single complaint was enough to warrant removing it from the county system. If the issue had been that the content had been too sexual or too anti-religious, I would have had stronger feelings. But my job was not to respond to a complaint if I agreed or disagreed, it was to resolve it according to our process.

The process moved the book from my hands to the branch supervisor and the county head of services, both had already stated that it was a selected book and was clearly marked as a fantasy, so what was the problem. Meanwhile, the parent asked me what was happening each time she came in, and I replied that the book was being reviewed – which was true. I wanted to have a strong belief and conviction that we were "right" in our decision to not remove the book from the shelf, but I was also aware that a parent has every right to protect their child from danger or harm, which she clearly believed the book represented.

So, in football terms, I punted. I didn't remove the book from the county system or ban it outright, I simply sent it to another branch. With almost thirty branches in the system and only four copies of the book, the odds were that we would not see it again, and the parent would be satisfied. I did tell her the book was gone, but didn't elaborate. She didn't press and seemed happy that the process "worked." I was never sure if I should feel that I won one, or lost one, or more importantly, if censorship had hurt a potential reader's opportunity to embrace the story. I tried to imagine a troubled six-year-old boy who wanted to flatten a tormentor and could do so safely through the pages of the book. It would be a form of bibliotherapy.

Ten years later the *Flat Stanley* books appeared, but I never heard of any of those causing a parental complaint.

Arvin, CA Public Library – J. Bradley

I'm not comfortable being preachy, but more people need to start spending as much time in the library as they do on the basketball court.

Kareem Abdul-Jabbar

CHAPTER 15 – **KING JAMES**

Children and books are a natural library connection. The introduction to literacy and the opportunity it brings for the future have always been recognized as a valuable contribution to society. Librarians understand this connection and nurture it with a variety of programs. Story times, book talks, summer reading clubs, and library visits are all used to promote the love of books, reading, and learning. Parents and teachers who bring their charges to the library wisely recognize the connection between literacy, learning, and life success.

But teachers, and parents are not our children's only role models, so when I heard from my son, that Miami Heat basketball star, LeBron James was shown reading books, I was thrilled. LeBron (aka King James) can reach children who aren't already library patrons, and who might not pay attention to the usual adults who talk about books.

My son is an NBA fan who follows the game avidly. When the Miami Heat won the championship in 2012, he called me to chat about it. One thing he noted after commiserating that our own Lakers didn't have a great year, was that LeBron had played brilliantly and deserved to be considered the best basketball player of the year. Of particular interest was that LeBron was shown reading books before the playoff games!

LeBron never attended college, going straight into the NBA after high school, so many fans were surprised to learn that he decided to read books to improve his focus before important games. There was *The Hunger*

Games, Catching Fire, and *Mockingjay* in the trilogy by Suzanne Collins, *Who Moved my Cheese*, Spencer Johnson's self-help book, and *The Pact,* a novel about three boys from tough neighborhoods deciding to go to college and become doctors. One beautiful fact was that LeBron read a great variety of books of his own and other's choosing.

ESPN's Michael Wilbon wrote, "Where cynics saw a ballplayer doing something for the cameras, I saw a chance, whatever LeBron's motivation, for a role model to use his influence to make an impact, intentional or not.... If LeBron is reading, then reading must be fairly cool. Is there a better message the world's best basketball player could send?" I am one of many who agree.

Along a similar vein, the American Library Association years ago developed a "Read" campaign that featured celebrities from the worlds of science, sports and entertainment to promote reading. Each poster and bookmark featured a celebrity, such as Oprah Winfrey, Steven Hawking, Los Lonely Boys, Keira Knightly, Orlando Bloom, Yao Ming, and Sasha Cohen. The names and faces changed over time as new faces emerged from sports, music, television, and cinema, but the message was always the same: a simple **Read!**

I'm excited that LeBron James is a new face with the same important message. So, from me, and others it's all hail the King. Three cheers for LeBron.

Hip-hip-hooray!

Hip-hip-hooray!

Hip-hip-hooray!

twitterphoto

Spiro, OK Branch Library - R. Pendleton

Children are made readers on the laps of their parents.

Emilie Buchwald

CHAPTER 16 – **PARENTS**

When I started collecting story hour books, one day early in my tenure as branch librarian, I took my first really detailed look at the picture book collection. Previously I'd settled for getting rid of the worst offenders (those with actual peanut butter on the pages, or notes like "missing pages noted 4/11/77") but today for some reason (including the nagging realization that, as *Madeline*'s Miss Clavell would say, Something Is Not Right) I knew I needed to do some work.

The previous librarian did not like children. Why else Small, Medium, Large, so that you had to use the catalog in order to find, for example, all of the *Curious George* books because they were on separate shelves? Why else would she have filed the children's fiction all along the aisle across from the adult non-fiction? It takes a brave child to crouch in that aisle while grownups are stumbling over him.

I knew we had some rather peculiar books in the picture book collection and I had formed a half-plan of moving them to a Parents' Shelf. I have no idea how big this shelf may become — I was only in the middle of H — but I was stunned. Imagine your toddler having her first experience with the library. Attracted by the pretty colors of the books she pulls out *The Fall of Freddy The Leaf*. This book explains death in an extended metaphor which ends with Freddy falling to the ground right after the first frost.

I won't even mention the holiday books we have already dispatched, including two or three where Jewish children learn that Santa Claus is not for them.

Today I found, among other treasures *Fly Away Home* by Eve Bunting. "My dad and I live in an airport.

That's because we don't have a home and the airport is better than the streets. We are careful not to get caught." That's the text on the first page of this picture book.

A couple of shelves over, there was *Not in here, Dad!* by Cheryl Dutton. Dad keeps trying to find a place to smoke, but we learn about all the awful stuff it does to your lungs and your teeth and your social life.

There was a lovely-looking picture book called something like *Time To Go* about what happens when your family farm is foreclosed and you have to sell everything off and move. The last page shows the boy with tears on his face.

Other tempting goodies include *Grandfather died Today, I had a Friend named Peter,* and, chillingly, *At Home with Daddy*. Oh, also, *"My Mother Travels a Lot".*

I repeat, I'm only to the middle of H.

First step, they go to my office, to the Parents' shelf. Second step, I'll decide whether to re-catalog them into children's non-fiction which is at least less deceptive.

Possible third step, they go

Out The Door.

I can't imagine what we have done to children who, accustomed to delight, find despair and sorrow and no hope. I'm getting these out of the way so our littles can find *Frances* and *Little Bear* and *Lilly with her Purple Plastic Purse* and *Little Toot* and — of course — *Madeline.*

Carthage, MO Public Library – R. Pendleton

Before they read words, children are reading pictures.

David Wiesner

CHAPTER 17 – **ROTTEN**

Today an unfamiliar mother came in after lunch,
(she's a Navy officer's wife - I just hadn't previously
met her) with her toddler daughter, a stroller son and
a big belly. The children had just come from getting
chicken pox shots because of the impending birth —

mom had checked with flight surgeon father-in-law, the local military surgeon and the pediatrician who agreed it was good.

The stroller baby fretted. The toddler examined the picture books (I was hoping she was staying toward the beginning of the alphabet). I went over to tell them about the story hour.

I said something banal to the toddler, who could not have been named Olivia, but that's what I remember as her name. Something like "Are you finding a good book?"

Olivia sensibly ignored me and kept going on her examination. At that point I wasn't aware that she had 15 minutes to select three books; it's a family rule.

"Olivia," her mother said, "the adult asked you a question."

Olivia kept on with her work.

"Olivia," her mother repeated. "The adult spoke to you. What do you say?"

I was feeling very bad.

"I am picking out a book," said Olivia.

"Ma'am," prompted her mother.

"I am picking out a book, ma'am," said Olivia and

turned her back and resumed work.

"Boo," said the stroller baby.

"Book," said the mom.

"Boo," said the stroller baby. Mom shook her head.

Olivia had already selected *Shy Charles* by Rosemary Wells.

I offered *Jessica,* by Kevin Henkes. I read a bit of it to Olivia and she grinned and grinned. Her mother added that to the stack, though I'm not sure how she will accept invisible playmates.

"We are making a chateau," Olivia announced to me.

Chateau? This child is three, max.

"They are studying France in her pre-school," said Mom. Oh. Must be Montessori. I offered *Madeline.*

"This is a story about a little girl who lives in Paris, France," I said, sounding dumb.

"Oh, Madeline," said Mom. She liked that too. I was doing fine.

Olivia handed over her real choice: *Rotten Ralph* (I forget the author. Ralph is a cat.)

"Oh, no," said mom, hastily thrusting it into my hands. She hadn't even opened it. "I don't think so. I don't want my child to hear That Word. If she hears it she will use it."

She then announced to Olivia that time was up, and Olivia formed up and marched to the circulation desk where I checked out the books in what I hoped was a sufficiently military manner. They then left ("Say good-bye to the adult, Olivia." "Good-bye." "Good-bye, ma'am." "Good-bye, ma'am." "Boo", said the stroller baby. "Boo, boo."), assuring me that they might well attend next week's story time.

OH DEAR I HOPE NOT.

Newburg, MO Public Library – R. Pendleton

There are many little ways to enlarge your child's world. Love of books is the best of all.

Jacqueline Kennedy

CHAPTER 18 - **MY FIRST STORY TIME**

Story time is one of the most treasured and valued of all library traditions. It introduces young children and their parents to the value of books and reading. Everyone seems to view it as one of the most important aspects of library work.

When you are a children's librarian, story time is one of your most important responsibilities, and one that you prepare for carefully. You choose a theme, perhaps animals, like bears, dogs, rabbits, or a holiday such as Valentines, Easter, Halloween or even Ground Hog Day. Seasons – Spring, Summer, Fall or Winter, or even something more specific like rain or wind are fun. The theme helps to determine the stories you will read and the activities you will offer. You can choose to offer a craft, game, play, film or fingerplay; you can even integrate dance or music into your event and use puppets or flannel boards. The creative types will find lots of fun ways to introduce children to books. I am not creative and the pressure is on.

Often story time is once a week on the same day and time and usually geared for three to five-year-olds. Some story times are offered in the evening hours when children are encouraged to come in their pajamas with their favorite doll or stuffed animal and can curl up with a blanket or on a mat or bean bag. If you have to entertain older children, you often read from one book and complete it over a period of time. It helps if each chapter or segment can stand alone, but you can always give a brief summary of what happened "Previously, in *Black Beauty*..." to help children catch up if they missed some of the readings.

Knowing the importance of story time put pressure on me when I was faced with my very first story time. I knew other library staff, including my supervisor, and parents would be watching and evaluating. I was nervous for several reasons. One, I wasn't really properly trained in children's work – I was a fraud. Sure, I had an MLS and was familiar with a lot of books, but I never took a Children's Literature class. My excuse was that I trained first to teach in high school, not elementary, so was expected to be a subject specialist in history and English not to work with kindergarten through eighth grade. Secondly, in library school I didn't believe there would be a job in public or school libraries – Proposition 13 had just passed in California, and budgets were being cut – and so I concentrated on the technical library where I thought I'd work and never be exposed to children's literature.

Another reason for my fear was my lack of experience in presenting certain materials in a public setting. I could read a book aloud but feared I would drop it while turning pages and balancing it, as I was, well - klutzy. I also saw that there was a puppet stage where I might be expected to demonstrate some puppetry. I have a small voice and small hands and, again, I lack coordination, so this posed a problem. I did have experience with my own children as I had read to them at bedtime every night from the time they were very young. I hoped that would help me select suitable books, but what would I do about the rest? How would I keep so many young children occupied and not allow them to run screaming around the library? I knew from experience how easily that could happen, and I worried that I would end up running after some while the rest of them grew restless and impatient. Who could blame them?

I decided to ask my supervisor for support. She explained the process that she used and reassured me that I didn't have to do puppets if I wasn't comfortable with them. I was somewhat relieved but not at all relaxed. I was still going to be watched by far too many adults. This was not like teaching in high school where I knew more than all the kids and I could easily stall or fake it if there was a tough question. I decided to follow her basic formula: A little exercise and a fingerplay to get the children settled on the floor, then a brief book to grab them. Follow that with a longer story and another interlude where kids did a stretch or a brief physical activity – think "I'm a Little Teapot," or "Old MacDonald had a Farm." Next present a flannel board story where the audience could participate and finish with another short punchy story. Hopefully that would take up the allotted half hour. Thirty minutes would go very quickly or very slowly and painfully.

The theme was a tough decision, but I went with one that was tried and true – bears. There were many good books to choose from, and some had the advantage of being favorites that the children and parents already know and like. I looked at *Goldilocks and the Three Bears*, *The Berenstain Bears*, *Brown Bear, Brown Bear*, *Corduroy*, *Little Bear*, *Winnie the Pooh*, and selected a few plus some back ups, then added *Going on a Bear Hunt*, for the physical activity that we would use. I learned some classic fingerplays to get the children seated with hands in their laps so they would be ready to listen to the stories.

The toughest part for me was to develop the pieces for the flannel board story. Since my cut and paste skills hadn't been used for many years, and my artistic ability was almost zero, I feared that the colored pieces of felt meant to be bears, chairs, beds and cereal bowls would look like blobs – and they did, until I learned to use magic marker and outline to emphasize the items. When all else failed I found pictures to trace and color and glued them to felt. At least you could tell that one was the bear and not the chair.

I thought I was ready. I hoped for the best. I wore bright colors because I had learned that children would rather look at red than plain walls. I added some other picture books around the room so that bored children could look, and hopefully all would be inspired to check out some books to take home. Then I waited nervously for the children and parents to arrive. I hoped for enough to make a good showing, but not too many so that they would be easier to manage and not misbehave.

The time finally arrived and the children and parents wandered into the room. Most seemed to know the process and sat down on the floor and faced the chair where I was seated. It seemed like a manageable size. I introduced myself and began with the fingerplay. The stories went well, no bones were broken, no blood was shed, the parents seemed pleased, and the library staff smiled. Whew, it was over, and I had survived. I could report back that 12 youngsters and their parents attended. Not a record, but certainly not a disgrace. It seemed to be a success.

Now, I'd probably be braver and ask the children's names. It's nicer to be able to associate a name with a face at any age. Now, I wouldn't be afraid to ask a parent to take a child who was too young, too ill-behaved, or too disruptive out of the room, but then, I was more into hope and prayer for all to go well. Now, I'd recognize that it would never be a perfect process, but it would be enjoyable for all, if I could relax and help them have fun.

After thirty-plus years I no longer give story times on a regular basis, but I volunteer for a library whose budget can no longer support one individual just to do children's programs. I give story times and truly enjoy it. I'm not afraid to try new craft projects with the kids – we can always wash hands, and it's fun to have a memento for them to take home and show off. I'm not afraid to offer food, although I do it only with the parent's knowledge and permission. I do fewer films and flannel board stories, but I have tried a few small puppets. I do more where the children can take part in the story and I talk more with them as individuals. The more I know about them, the more fun we have together. I may see some of them only once, but it is a joy to see them around town and be recognized as a story lady.

The wonderful part of the experience is that most children become completely engrossed in the books and are very enthusiastic. Although there is the occasional issue with some who are too young or too old, for the most part story time is magical. It brings children and books together and starts the process where they learn to read and love books.

Construction at Atascadero, CA Public Library – S. Bradley

Santa Claus is anyone who loves another and seeks to make them happy;

Edwin Osgood Grover

CHAPTER 19 -**SANTA**

Our library system, with its two dozen branches spread throughout the County, owned a Santa Claus suit which was put to use lavishly during the holiday season. It would travel in the Library van from branch to branch, sometimes appearing two or three times in a day depending on story time schedules. It was getting a bit limp, and experienced branch managers would try their best to schedule their Santa visit early in the season, but as the newest branch librarian I found myself toward the end of the list.

But we had plenty to worry about without thinking about fashion. Our library was in a very mixed neighborhood, including some homes of field workers far below any poverty line, so we made sure to beg candy and fruit and whatever else we could get from our local merchants as goody bags for the children. Our children's librarian spent several December story times making snowflakes and colored-paper Christmas trees for the children to take home as well.

Three days before our big Santa visit, we learned that our regular Santa, a loyal Friends of the Library member, had been taken ill and couldn't attend. Our situation was dire.

I did what any mother would do under the circumstances: I bribed, threatened and coerced my sixteen-year-old son, Phil, to substitute. I forget what I offered but I know that a new skateboard figured into the mix.

The Santa suit was designed for a portly middle-aged

tallish man. Phil was a skinny middle-sized shy teenager, but with a red stocking cap, a wig and beard of marvelously false white cotton batting and a sturdy belt around his middle to hold the pants up, he was, as even he admitted, unrecognizable.

We had a full house for this story time. We began with some songs and a story, to which nobody paid any attention, and then Santa appeared. He entered the room and stood for a few moments looking at the children. I was afraid he was going to either faint or throw up, but when he realized that they were calling, "Hi, Santa, Hi, Santa," he gathered up his bag and went to his special chair. The plan was for him to take each child on his knee, like they do in department stores, and hear their Christmas wish, and give each a goody bag.

All went humming along. The tiniest children just wanted to pat his knee, others wanted to talk to this strange Santa.

Suddenly I realized that the room had become very quiet. Turning to the door I saw that we had a half dozen additional children. The boys from the group home had come in.

This group home was a board and care facility for seriously disturbed and/or handicapped boys, who were all between the ages of ten and fifteen; some were as large as Phil. They made us nervous when they visited the library because they had so much energy and so few library, or social, skills.

Now they lined up against the wall and watched Santa. Phil soldiered on, concentrating on the children already in line. Before we knew it, the big boys had joined the end of the line. At first the smaller children poked each other and eyed them nervously, but they caught on before we did.

The boys from the group home believed.

It was not easy for these tall boys to climb onto Phil's lap but each one managed it, one after the other. And not one child laughed or teased them. And each of the boys said, more or less, "thank you Santa," as they received their goody bags.

That was the climax and the finish of that Christmas story time. We sent all of our guests home, each one clutching at least one treat. Phil divested himself of his Santa gear and re-packed it. And we did what that library has done for year: we took down the library Christmas tree, stowing its decorations for next year, and set it outside the back door, just around the corner from the windows in a dark spot, where someone who really needed a Christmas tree could find it.

SECTION 5:

POLICIES

Sycamore IL, Public Library – R. Pendleton

If a public library is doing its job, it has something that offends every single person.

Phyliss A. Salak, *American Libraries,* April 1993

CHAPTER 20 - **DROWNING**

I had been a reference librarian for a little more than a year when our cataloger and Head of Technical Services retired and I took over. This was during the final years of local cataloging, back in the innocent days when library staff created the catalog cards as part of the routine procedures of acquiring new materials. We would receive new books, catalog them, process them by jacketing them and inserting the security strips and pockets, and file the catalog cards.

Most of our time was taken up with the maintenance of the card catalog, but as I became more familiar with the Technical Services Department I realized that we had another, larger problem: we were drowning in books.

It makes sense, after all. The library had a generous book budget. Each week we received a half-dozen or more large cartons of books. But we had no procedures for removing books from our collection.

Each librarian was assigned one or two sections of Dewey Decimal Numbers and we weeded our sections continually. The discarded books – those with outdated or wildly inaccurate information, damaged or mutilated, extra copies of former but now ignored best sellers – would be hauled downstairs to the stacks in the basement. There they would sit. Apparently forever.

The library's financial structure listed books as capital asset. This meant, according to the city finance people, that each book was a permanent asset of the library, thus of the city, and removing it was a complex process. Obviously this was an impossible dilemma, but my predecessor had developed a plan.

The books were stamped WITHDRAWN, the cards were pulled from the catalog, and the books were packed into boxes – liquor boxes, the empty cartons from our book jobber, boxes gather or coaxed from other departments – which were stacked along the back wall. When the stack became too large, we would notify General Services.

Then one morning a City pickup truck would pull into our loading dock, and we would push and shove and haul our boxes into the truck bed. The truck would then take them to the city landfill where they would be buried. The important thing was that nobody outside our department was supposed to know what we were doing. My supervisor made sure I knew that this was supposed to be a deep secret, because we didn't want to give the impression that we were disposing of important city assets. I had the distinct impression that if word got out, my nascent library career would be finished.

I managed to ignore the whole business for months, but one day I realized that it would only get worse, so I arranged for a pickup. We lined up book carts loaded with boxes, and as soon as the truck arrived we made a kind of bucket brigade, emptying our book carts by dropping the boxes into the pickup truck below in the loading dock.

All went well until the truck, heavily loaded, began to drive away. A few boxes on top toppled over and a couple fell out of the truck completely, bouncing onto the pavement and bursting open, just about in front of City Hall.

What to do? I gathered my clerk Bea, who was strong, agile and closest to the door, and we raced for my VW Beetle. All the way along the road up the hill to the landfill, we followed the truck. Bea would jump out each time we saw a box or a book, and throw them into the car – not easy in a VW Bug. Fortunately, it was mid-morning on a weekday when most people were at work, at home or in school.

After what seemed like days but was really probably about a half-hour, we reached the landfill and added our contributions to the pile, then returned to the library to learn whether our cover had been blown.

Fortunately for all concerned, our new city librarian realized, as I had, that this was an untenable situation. If anybody had ever tried to audit the Library, I don't know what we would have done about the missing thousands of books (as far as I know, this procedure had been in place for at least fifteen years). She managed, after hard work, to re-write the library budget so that books were counted as Supplies rather than Assets, and we happily continued to maintain the collection without worrying about being arrested for theft.

Cerro Coso Community College, CA Library – J. Bradley

Borrowers of books -- those mutilators of collections, spoilers of the symmetry of shelves, and creators of odd volumes.

Charles Lamb

CHAPTER 21 - **ESPIONAGE**

My first job behind the library desk was in the reference department of a mid-sized public library. It was before the days of desktop computers, when life seemed fairly predictable. We found materials for our patrons and the circulation department checked them out. For the small number of home-bound patrons, the Friends of the Library delivered their book requests and collected new requests. The most exciting part of the work was answering reference questions: McDonald's was running a trivia contest when I started working, and we enjoyed hunting for the odd and strange answers in addition to working on the usual wide range of questions.

In addition to our reference work, each of was assigned a section of the Dewey Decimal System, for us to manage. We read reviews and proposed new items, and checked our part of the library stacks to see what needed to be mended, replaced or updated. My sections included the 940s, including World War II. Like all libraries, we had a large and popular collection of World War II books, in such frequent use that we regularly found some that had simply worn out. I had been working away at learning my section for a few months when I began to notice a problem. One of our regular patrons was writing in the books.

Many library users like to make marks in the books they read. One of our home-bound patrons would put a tiny check mark underneath the author's name of each mystery he read, so that he wouldn't re-read them. Another patron marked a number, from one to ten, near the gutter on the inside back cover of each book; this was his Enjoyment Rating (I found that even though I didn't know who was doing this, my tastes were the same, so whenever I found a number 6 or higher, I would check it out knowing I would probably enjoy it).

But my World War II reader had crossed the line. He may have begun by underlining the odd phrase, or noting an unfamiliar word, but now he had begun to comment on the writing itself. In heavy pencil and large letters. "Not True!" "IT WAS THE 38TH BRIGADE, FOOL!" In some cases he wrote over the printed text, making it almost impossible to read. His pencil dug into the paper so that even if the words were erased, the marks could still be read. More uncomfortably, he was intent on defending the SS and Gestapo, supporting the Final Solution.

I found myself removing several books each time I checked the shelves. They were old and shabby but well-regarded histories, so I requested re-orders. But shortly I realized that he was such an insatiable—and opinionated—reader that we could spend the bulk of our book budget just supplying him with new fodder. This was during the 1970s when libraries and public buildings received occasional bomb threats and we were all just a little bit on edge (in our city, when the library received a bomb threat, the reference librarian on duty was required to accompany the police into the library to look for bombs).

When I brought an armload of defaced books to my boss, the City Librarian, she agreed that we had a serious problem. The question was how to solve it. We had no idea who the culprit might be.

One of the most widely respected policies in public library work, one for which even the mildest-mannered librarian will speak up, protest and even go to jail for, is patron privacy. If you are an adult owning a library's borrowing card, the record of the books you have borrowed does not exist so long as you return your books when they are due. Obviously, this makes catching a repeat offender difficult if not impossible. We decided that, although this principal was enforced for rule-obeying patrons, our culprit had lost his privileges because of his vandalism. We would do our best to identify him and punish him.

So my boss threw herself into this project. She first enlisted the support of the circulation desk staff by showing them the marked-up books. They discussed the handwriting and speculated about whether the same handwriting would show up on library card applications. Since for many borrowers the circulation desk staff are the only points of contact, our culprit might have engaged them in discussions of politics or warfare or made Anti-Semitic remarks. But nothing came to mind.

Then she discussed the problem with the reference desk staff, covering the same bases. Nobody remembered talking to any patron about these subjects, or recognizing the handwriting, although it was quite distinctive—the letters were printed with capitals much larger than the rest of the word, each letter slanting just a bit forward. Everybody checked books in their own sections, but only World War Two seemed to be attacked.

We took to wandering through the 900s, noticing anybody who might be studying the section in question. Somebody suggested making a display of provocative books to see who took any special interest. The Interlibrary Loan clerk reported that there were no outstanding requests for World War II material.

During the next several weeks, many books were returned with the same kind of writing. Whoever was checking them out was working hard. We scared each other with speculations about serial vandals, and unbalanced individuals who were "getting worse".

Books were returned to the library via the outdoor book drop or a slot in the front of the circulation desk, or, rarely, placement on the circ desk counter. It was not practical to spy on our patrons—at least not directly.

The police and the city attorney were polite but absolutely not interested in participating in our project. We couldn't blame them: so far the only damage was to the books, and many of them were getting older and shabbier anyway.

Suddenly, the problem seemed to stop. For about a month no mutilated books were returned (the circ desk staff had been told to riffle the pages of each returned book, which made them grumpier than usual). We wondered what had happened. Had the culprit become ill, gone on vacation, died? Had he simply tired of the project? Did he think he had spread his message and could relax?

But at a Monday morning staff meeting, the head of Circulation reported that he was back. A patron had brought in a big bag of returned books, saying he had just come back from a month's visit to Washington, D. C., where he had been house hunting. Now he was preparing to move there, so he had rounded up all of his library books because he was beginning to pack.

Aha! We now knew who he was—an ordinary-looking, unexceptional, regular patron. We agreed that we never would have thought him guilty of this—either the behavior or the creepy thought patterns.

But the circ desk had processed the returned books, so now we had no proof of his connection to the marked-up books. And of course there was no record of his borrowing any specific titles, which would give us his name.

So in most respects we were back where we started, except that we were hopeful that the book mutilation was finished. Our Librarian was still worried, though, because we had, she felt, unleashed a villain upon the libraries of Washington, D.C. She still had unfulfilled responsibilities.

After some careful thought, she settled upon a strategy that made us all feel better: With the aid of the A.L.A. Directory and a map of the area, she wrote to the librarian in charge of each library, warning them about the danger to their World War II books. If you have a new resident applying for a card, she told them, and he says he comes from [our town], then just watch out. Despite her hard work, we continued to feel a bit nervous for quite awhile, and we never did learn whether he was a repeat offender.

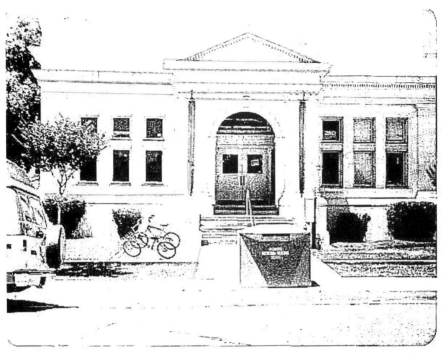

Baker Branch, Kern County, CA Library – R. Pendleton

A library implies an act of faith.

Victor Hugo

CHAPTER 22 - **MURDERER**

When I started my first library job, our city librarian was a charming, soft-spoken, absent-minded woman on the verge of retirement, who thought about library finances only when forced to do so. Naturally she was replaced by a more businesslike manager.

Our new boss may not have been a scholar, or even

much of a reader, but she had a sharp eye for pleasing her employer. She participated actively in committees of the city government and attended as many (cheap or free) community activities as she could squeeze into her work schedule. The staff approved highly of this because the community activities took her away from the library for hours on end, and her ambitions actually helped the library become more visible.

This was during the time when management training philosophy said that if you could manage one department you could manage them all, and we heard that we'd eventually be rotated around through Fire and Police and Sewers and the like (fortunately for us, that never happened, although after serious City Hall study the reference librarian job was equated with Assistant Tree Trimmer).

She worked hard to make the library cost-effective and developed presentations to demonstrate that rather than being a drag on the budget, the library actually brought in income. If you did not live within the city limits, you had to pay a non-resident fee to get any services at all, including answers to reference questions; we had to follow up on large fines and unpaid fees through Small Claims Court; she tried to institute rental charges for our conference room, but that never worked; she spent more and more of the book budget on rental books.

Her zeal to maximize library revenues reached a peak one summer day when we learned that the City Treasurer had been arrested for the murder of his wife. The story which spread through the library was that he had returned home unexpectedly for lunch but found his wife in bed with one of his friends, whereupon he dispatched her and called the police to surrender (the ultimate result has vanished from my memory).

When the City Librarian heard the story she was horrified. "But he was here, in the library, that very morning! And he checked out several books! I saw him!"

Whereupon she strode off to the police department and made her claim to the library materials. That very afternoon she accompanied a police officer to the accused's home where she gathered up the books. No doubt they would have been returned anyway, but she loved to tell the story and took credit for her quick work.

Please read this declaration aloud when asked

I hereby undertake not to remove from the library, or to mark, deface, or injure in anyway, any volume, document, or other object belonging to it or in its custody: not to bring into the Library or kindle therein any fire or flame, and not to smoke in the Library: and I promise to obey all rules of the Library.

Bodleian Library, University of Oxford

CHAPTER 23 - **RULES**

In an ideal world we would need no library rules. Everyone using a library would have common goals and want to use the library for a "good" purpose. They would want the library to be a nice place to visit, and would not disrupt other patrons or staff. They would wish only to use the library to access its resources, and they would respect and maintain those resources. Unfortunately, we do not live in such a world. So, we have rules.

We have rules to keep users – especially children, safe. We have rules that help to safeguard and maintain the collection. Some rules protect staff from danger or harassment. Librarians are committed to protect the rights of patrons to read what they want without undue fear that their choices will be made public, much like HIPA protects an individual's health information. Library rules protect privacy while other rules are added based on unforeseen incidents, or sadly because some individuals won't act reasonably without a written "rule" or regulation.

Most library rules are logical and sensible. Smoking, food, and drink are usually prohibited in public areas, and areas where materials are kept. Large bags, and packages may be inspected or stored. The length of time items may be borrowed is limited, and failure to return them in that time usually results in a fine. If any items are lost or damaged, financial charges may result.

The digital age has brought computers into libraries with a whole new set of rules.

Computers must often be reserved, and limited to library-card holders. The time period is monitored and the ability to access music, games, emails, or to print may also be controlled. Adding or deleting programs is not allowed and problems must be reported to the staff. Access to materials deemed as inappropriate (obscene or pornographic) may not be permitted. In children's areas even stricter filtering of online materials often occurs.

By and large most users accept and understand rules.

They recognize the need to add rules and adjust them. But still there is the exceptional case that has resulted in the more stringent and explicit rules. The sad truth is that imposing long lists of rules and prohibitions often makes people seek out the one thing that is not specifically forbidden. That is why many libraries have had to include rules that specifically prohibit behaviors regarding nudity, sexual behavior, body odor, and use of the lavatories as bathrooms and laundries.

Most librarians I know would probably like to make some rules of their own to govern the library users. I suspect we'd agree on implementing some of the following rules and punishments.

1. 20 minutes in a chilly dunk tank to wake up those who bring in children and leave or totally ignore them while they run, yell, bump into others and smear unknown substances on books and surfaces.

2. 30 minutes in a room with a rabid pit bull to those (not researching breast cancer) who ogle naked boobs online while snickering and/or drooling.

3. 2 hours of etiquette training repeated until the material is understood as evidenced by passing a test, for those who exhibit any of the following:

    a. Sniffling, coughing, and otherwise spreading germs through the air without the use of hankies or covering one's mouth and nose.

b. Excessive time spent on loud phone conversations particularly those that include arguments, or sharing of personal data.

c. Using the library as one's personal office space making it impossible for others to reach or use the nearby resources.

d. Telling staff members that their taxes pay the staff's salary, after bragging about being so smart they didn't pay any taxes.

e. Rudeness of any sort

On the other hand, some rules and signs seem to tell a story –*Like these two.*

PLEASE

KEEP THE DOOR CLOSED

DURING MEETINGS

SO THAT BATS DO NOT

COME INTO THE BUILDING

Thank You

THE NEWSPAPERS AND MAGAZINES

ARE PROVIDED FOR EVERYONE TO

READY AND ENJOY. HOWEVER, TO

THOSE OF YOU WHO ARE TEARING OUT

PAGES AND TAKING THE

NEWSPAPERS AND MAGAZINES; BE

ADVISED THAT ACCORDING TO CITY

ORDINANCE 7.0502 THIS IS **THEFT**

AND YOU MAY BE FINED UP TO $200

AND/OR JAILED FOR UP TO 30 DAYS .

A COPY MACHINE IS AVAILABLE TO

MAKE COPIES OF ARTICLES OF

INTEREST TO YOU.

Yes, there is a place for library rules, **but** I wish we didn't need any.

SECTION 6:

LIBRARY PATRONS

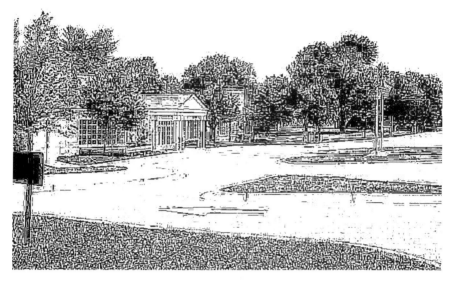

Herbert Hoover Library, Iowa City, IA – R. Pendleton

A good library will never be too neat, or too dusty, because somebody will always be in it, taking books off the shelves and staying up late reading them.

Lemony Snicket

CHAPTER 24 - **E.T.**

The library staff called him E. T. Not that he was an alien, but he was so strange, and those happened to be his initials, so that is what he became. He was a fixture in the library of the small University of California campus and could often be found snoring away on one of their comfortable couches.

Every library has its share of waifs and strays. Public libraries have the larger numbers, because they are public buildings; people who behave with reasonable decorum cannot be kept away. But universities and colleges also seem to be targets of people like E. T. Somehow people who cannot seem to find their way across the street eventually show up at the library, ready to spend every free hour there.

Although the library was his favorite spot, E. T. knew his way around campus and visited other offices including the registrar, and the occasional classroom. The staff put up with him if he didn't cause trouble, but called security when he threatened them or disrupted regular business. After he accosted the library director in the gym, he was prohibited from using the library; after all, he wasn't even a student.

The seriously strange are a powerful subject for staff conversation at break time. Sharing stories about odd behavior offers a kind of strength in dealing with people who may appear threatening, or perhaps just peculiar. In our children's department, for example, we realized that one middle-aged man was appearing every day after school. Always clad in the same purple velvet blazer, he occupied a seat near the picture books, bringing a newspaper which he spread across his lap but never seemed to read. It took our director several repetitions of "Adults are not permitted to sit in the primary department" (a rule she apparently made up for the situation) before he left the toddlers and returned to the adult side of the library.

E. T. must have learned something from his campus wanderings. When he found out that students had privileges, he decided to enroll. He may have had good high school grades or scored well on tests, or found the right guidance counselor. Perhaps he was a veteran who used his benefits for education. Whatever the reason, he became a student, attended classes and was allowed back into the library.

We always resented the appearance of people like E. T., because it meant that in addition to everything else we were doing, we had to keep a sharp eye on him. And while he stood out with his unwashed hair and odd wardrobe, there were others harder to catch. For example, a small but determined group of women planted religious tracts inside our books for months. These were brightly illustrated pamphlets with horrifying descriptions of diseases and torments. Checking through returned books and trying to spot the culprits took more time than we had to spare, so we finally decided to give up, and let our patrons throw the pamphlets away when they found them.

E. T.'s behavior was similar. Enrolled in a history class he told the professor that he should teach them about the Lost City of Atlantis. When the instructor refused because that wasn't part of the curriculum, E.T. became very angry and threatened to report him to the college trustees and the chancellor. He became noisy and disruptive in other classes as well, and soon flunked out of school.

He remained a frequent visitor to the library, however. The staff would help him as long as he was reasonable. Finally we realized that several months had passed without a visit. Where had he gone? Where is he now? Had he fulfilled the promise of his initials and returned to outer space.

Trois Riveres, Quebec Library – R. Pendleton

No place affords a more striking conviction of the vanity of human hopes than a public library.

Samuel Johnson - *The Rambler.* March 23, 1751

CHAPTER 25 – **THE FLASHER**

My first encounter with a library flasher was not face to face – or worse. I was young and naïve and would have found it a problem. I was in my twenties and working as a library bibliographic assistant in an academic library. At the time, computers were not used for daily tasks, and did not sit on everyone's desk; they were reserved for the large and important work dictated by the faculty. Computers were physically so large that they occupied entire rooms of their own. As a result, many library tasks were done by hand by lowly assistants. We might have college degrees but not the master's degree which signified the professional librarian.

I was such an assistant, helping to earn the family income while benefiting from the college's policy that helped cover my husband's graduate school tuition. We were twenty or thirty library assistants who helped select, purchase and catalog books. We enjoyed a friendly camaraderie and social life of lunches and the occasional party. Most of our group were young women, usually single although some of us were married and a few even had children. We developed the kind of relationships that came with surviving poor pay, few benefits, and shared hopes for a better future.

Our friendships didn't often include intimate details, but some little tidbits were shared now and then that added to our knowledge of life, sex and opened our eyes to experiences. When Anna revealed she had experimented and contracted crabs, we were shocked but titillated. If William shared some of his gay adventures, we giggled. But we didn't know what went on in someone's private life if they weren't vocal about it, and most of us were on the shy side.

Of the group, two of the quieter ones were the best friends Kim and Bella. Kim was Japanese-American and had been selected to work with the main computer interface to the library. We didn't know the details but knew it was important work. She was viewed as somewhat elite because of her position, and because she could travel around campus, and not be tied to her desk. Her one little eccentricity was that each December 7 she celebrated Pearl Harbor day and went out for martinis.

Bella was a short, young Hispanic woman, married with a baby. She was tied to her desk and worked closely with Kim. Bella's reputation was that she was a bright, tireless worker, who could decipher the complicated numbers that composed the library's purchasing system and keep her incompetent boss from total chaos. We saw her beautiful baby girl once in a while, when her husband, a tall good-looking African American brought her to visit while running errands.

The library assistants enjoyed a comfortable routine based on the budget year and purchasing schedule. We had to depend upon each other for news and changes in routine. We did a good job of sharing when we had something of interest.

Then we heard of the flasher.

The flasher was first encountered one winter evening in a remote wing of the library when he exposed himself to a sophomore who was studying late. Her report didn't filter down to us until mid-morning when we heard a vague version that didn't have any fun details. We asked, but apparently the library leadership didn't want to frighten students, parents, and the important alumni donors by spreading any details. Without more news we had to let it drop.

The first sighting was assumed to be a one-of-a-kind event, that didn't really impact us. We didn't work at night, and it was far from our work area. The student was apparently not traumatized by the event, because the flasher was moving away from her and she never felt threatened. Some people assumed she was lying and may have needed a study break, or some sympathy from her professors.

The flasher didn't reappear for several months.

The second sighting was longer, and we felt more involved. Perhaps we could identify or help capture him, now that we had a good description. The flasher was tall, and wore dark clothing and a long jacket. He appeared in the early evening and stayed long enough to see his victim's reaction. She was a screamer and as other patrons and staff came to investigate, he disappeared into the stacks.

This time the library leadership had to react. They left the first sighting in the hands of campus security, but this time they contacted the police. We didn't see any sketches of the suspect but heard that young women were being warned not to study alone in the library at night. It was still very low key, but the second young woman was not a publicity hound and we felt bad that the first young woman had been treated so poorly.

We all wondered what we would do if we were flashed. Would we be afraid, scream, cry, or run? Could we get a good description? How do you describe a flasher? Would we have the presence of mind to even see his face or remember his features? It was fodder for lots of discussion. William gave us anatomically correct descriptors in case we ever saw him in the flesh.

Armed with our new knowledge, we were ready for an encounter. We knew the odds were not in our favor, but we hoped. If he appeared during work hours, we could help apprehend him. We tried to use police jargon as much as possible. We began to look for opportunities to search for books in the stacks – pretending to help with the cataloging of a new title. We carefully went around in pairs.

The flasher did not disappoint us. He showed up at 11 am in the stacks the following week and exposed himself to two female students. They raised an alarm and he was chased. He was fast and must have known his way around the library, because he escaped despite the students and guards searching for him.

We were amazed at his brazen attack. Didn't he know everyone was watching for him? How could he get away during the day? We heard more details about his appearance, although not the ones that we craved. He was at least six-foot-one, perhaps taller. He was African American, and wore chinos, a dark green t-shirt and a dark-light-weight jacket. He had no visible scars or tattoos, and was clean shaven with medium length hair. He could have been one of hundreds of students, or a resident of the surrounding neighborhood.

We had so much to talk about, it was a wonder any work was done, but we had deadlines and quotas, and we managed. Lunch and breaks were times of discussion of the flasher's daring or foolishness. We had different opinions of his motivation, and wondered at the meaning of the escalation of his attacks. He hadn't harmed anyone, but we worried that he could. For many young women it could be a traumatizing event, and suppose he began to do more than simply expose.

Days went by with no more news, and we moved

slowly back into our routines, while hoping for another attack or the capture that would satisfy our curiosity. The next Monday, news of the capture came, but our expected elation didn't.

The police had guessed at his entry and exit points and had personnel waiting when he came again. The man captured that Saturday was Bella's husband. Bella was not at her desk on Monday, and Kim was quieter than ever and didn't participate in any talk. There were no declarations of innocence, and the police were sure he was our flasher. We found that we were not excited or happy, but very sad that one of our own was hurting. Bella didn't deserve to have trouble in her life and we didn't want to add to her misery.

After a time, Bella returned to the library and we respected her privacy. No further discussion of the flasher was heard. We understood her husband went to prison, and we were sorry that she was alone. We never understood what the motivation for his flashing had been, but we learned he had been out of work – a detail never shared by Bella. Slowly, we returned to normal; we knew all was well on December 7th when Bella and Kim celebrated again with martinis.

Sackville, NB Public Library – R. Pendleton

*The public library is one of the few places left where
one can be private.*

Lawrence Clark Powell, *Arizona Highways,* Aug. 1960

CHAPTER 26 – **QUIET MAN**

I worked in a public library in a community that was
known for its lack of crime. We joked that the biggest
problem the past year was the theft of laundry off
Mrs. Smith's clothesline. Although we heard there
were drugs in the area and possibly some meth labs in
the nearby desert, we were generally a quiet sleepy
town. I also assumed all of the people were quiet too.

One young gentleman visited the library regularly. He

was quiet but not unpleasant, and appeared to be in his early to mid twenties. I always believed he must be a graduate student working on a thesis or a writer – perhaps creating the great American novel. He didn't borrow many books, but he spent hours sitting at a cubicle, writing and studying notes. He had been a regular for years but I don't think most of us even knew his name. He never caused trouble or asked for special attention, but obeyed all the rules and was easy to have around.

Because he was a regular, and used the same parking lot as the staff, we grew to know his car too. It was an older foreign model, perhaps 15 to 20 years old, but in good working condition, always starting and reliable. It wasn't shiny or detailed, but it was clean and unmarked by any dents.

One afternoon, when I was on the desk, another patron came in to report that she had backed into a car. She pointed out the quiet man's car. She didn't believe that she had caused damage, but wanted to report it to someone in case there was any issue. Because she had told me, I was responsible for seeing that it was reported. I looked at the cars and was sure that there would be no difficulty since they both looked fine. We looked carefully but saw no scratches, dents or damage of any kind. But, just to be doing the right thing, I asked her to wait while I told the quiet man of the incident.

I found him in his usual spot, and told him that someone had backed into his car, but it looked just fine. He looked alarmed and jumped up at once. He walked out to look at his car, and came back in where he saw the other woman driver.

That is when everything went terribly wrong. He became the Mr. Hyde to his former, Dr. Jekyll persona. He went postal! He screamed at her, and swore words that I couldn't imagine he had ever used before. As she wilted and became teary under his barrage, the quiet man became more angry and abusive, throwing books and papers around, and getting louder.

I was shocked, and dismayed. My supervisor, the rest of the staff, and most of the patrons came to watch the display. In order to defuse the situation, I told the woman that we had her information and she should just leave. I was worried the quiet man could work himself up to where he might hit her. In all the years he had been coming to the library, he had hardly uttered a word, but he was making up for it now.

After she left, he remained agitated and couldn't sit down. He walked around and muttered to himself, an entirely different person than the quiet man we were used to. He finally left, but after that we noticed he was never the same. He was agitated, swore under his breath, often walked around and stared at others, and didn't seem at all focused on his "work."

Later, one librarian who knew his family revealed that

he was mentally ill, and had never completed school, or held a job. The quiet man we had seen in the library was heavily medicated, and not the same man known by his family and friends. Perhaps the latest episode was due to a change in medication, or the current medication was no longer effective, but he was changed. After a few months of his new behavior, he disappeared, returning to the institution that had helped him to once function in society.

I learned more than I wanted to from the incident, and felt horrible that I played a part in it. I apologized to the woman patron the next time I saw her, and explained what I had learned about our quiet man. I now watched others more carefully, and never assumed that they would be reasonable if things went wrong. I learned not to judge the patrons by their look, just as I wouldn't judge a book by its cover.

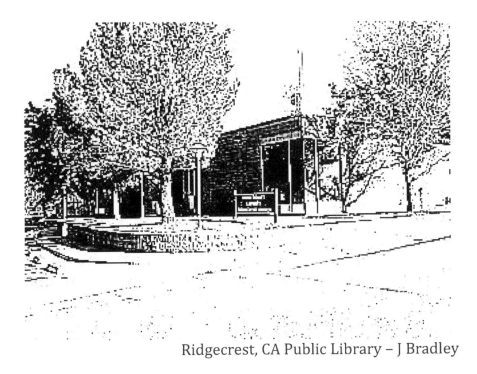

Ridgecrest, CA Public Library – J Bradley

There is not such a cradle of democracy upon the Earth as the Free Public Library -- this republic of letters, where neither rank, office, nor wealth receives the slightest consideration.

Andrew Carnegie

CHAPTER 27 – **WALNUT MAN**

In the 1980s I was a branch librarian in Bakersfield, California. My branch looked like a Carnegie Library. It was set on a small rise of ground with lawn all around. Steps led from the sidewalk to the base of the library, and more steps led up to the front door. This

Carnegie look-alike, designed locally a half century before I got there, was slated to become a Registered Historic Landmark, but during my tenure it was a small, shabby, overcrowded but well-loved branch serving a very mixed bag of residents.

Bakersfield is a major freight train station, traditionally a stopping point for men who grab rides in empty boxcars whenever security has turned its head. We were located just up the street from a men's homeless shelter which provided bed, breakfast and supper along with religious services. During the day the men were required to leave the building. They knew, and newcomers quickly learned, that the public library was nearby, free, open to all, warm in the winter and cool in the summer. While most of them made only short visits, usually in bad weather, some became our regular patrons. I wrote this in 1981:

Today was the first day of the winter rains. It was cold with a strong wind blowing the steady rain into faces and down shoe-tops. Puddles forming instantly in the hard-packed desert soil washed a summer's accumulation of old paper cups, gum wrappers and other detritus down the sidewalks and across the pitted library lawn, where they mingled with other awful nameless garbage.

By the time we had been open for an hour we noticed

that ten raggedy men had positioned themselves in chairs, each one gravely regarding a book or magazine.

We only have eighteen chairs in the whole public reading room.

The two youngest, each reading a Tarzan book, had stowed their backpacks neatly under the card catalog. An astoundingly handsome man, sort of a Paul Newman with Jerry Garcia's hair, was studying the *Fresno Bee* want ads.

Three undistinguished gentlemen with gray stubble were sharing a table, their bedrolls crammed under their chairs, with one of our regulars, The Man Who Twitches. As usual, he was totally oblivious to their presence.

A large happy-looking man wearing Big Mac overalls and a bright red stocking cap was drifting into sleep over his copy of the *Ladies Home Journal*.
An alert-looking old man with a long white beard and shoulder-length white hair had brought his own books carefully wrapped in a plastic sack.

The last was The Man With The Walnut, one of our regulars and a growing cause for concern. He stands about six and a half feet tall, or would if he ever stood up straight, and must weigh about 250 pounds or more. His clothes, which have been the same since summer, although becoming more and more dirty, are boots, brown serge pants, a plaid shirt covered by a blue windbreaker covered by a red windbreaker. That gives him a lot of pockets. Each pocket contains many precious objects, which he examines in a specific order – bottle caps, tiny pieces of paper, twigs and other less identifiable things.

On sunny days, he stops at the foot of the library steps, removes a walnut from his pocket, kisses it, blows on it, replaces it in his pocket, does the same with a penny, turns around three times, takes out a folded piece of paper and chants to it and then replaces it, turns around three more times and then enters the library. He searches for a book which he brings to his seat. He then opens the book, takes the walnut from his pocket, kisses it, blows on it, passes it over the page of the book then replaces it in his pocket. These actions are repeated every time he turns the page or chooses a new book, until he falls asleep.

On the one hand, we are happy to see him fall asleep quickly because he replaces the book in a place he himself chooses and after a particularly alert day our shelver has quite a few books to retrieve. On the other hand, when he falls asleep, he snores. Loudly.

It was one of the more orderly days at the library. Our new clientele having no doubt had previous training at other libraries knew exactly the standards of behavior expected of them. They sat quietly reading, occasionally wandering out to the relatively sheltered porch for a quick smoke. The white-haired gentleman spent an alarmingly long time in the restroom and came out looking rosy and gleaming, smelling of institutional soap.

But as the building warmed up, a certain odor began to permeate the place: wet wool steaming by the heaters, cigarette smoke blown in through the front door, and the unmistakable human aromas of people who haven't bathed in an extremely long time.

Library personnel being notoriously long-suffering, we did little except giggle nervously and keep our distance, although we did notice that our more conventional patrons seemed to hurry with their book selection.

The Man With The Walnut had drifted into an extremely deep sleep, occasionally snoring and grunting. Even the others regarded him with disdain, as though fearful that he was going to endanger their presence.

Around noon we got into a ferocious discussion about whether we could or should require people to leave for Sleeping In The Library (we can't).

By afternoon, when the rain still hadn't slackened, the aroma had reached an unmistakable level and the Walnut Man's snoring was joined by the Man in the Stocking Cap's soft sleeping sounds.

Women coming in for books stopped at the front door, sniffed, smiled, hustled about on their errands and occasionally paused to comment on the "poor souls", and then left quickly.

After school brought our usual influx of kids, who, streetwise, took in the situation at a glance and rather sympathetically kept a little quieter than usual, so as not to wake them. (Since the library is also located just up the street from Wino Park, our kids have grown up seeing folks sleeping in doorways or on the grass, and dropping off of freight trains).

One very small child who hadn't got the message wandered up to the Walnut Man, banged on his arm with her fist and said "Hey, hey, wake up," causing acute embarrassment to her mother and amusement to everyone else except the Walnut Man who woke briefly, kissed his walnut, turned the page of the book before him, and drifted back into slumber.

Finally our most motherly clerk, driven beyond endurance, brought out a giant can of Lysol air freshener and strode through the entire library spraying. Tactfully she began in the far back corners, but gradually the public area filled with the sound of hissing. The raggedy readers began to stir and sniff.

The two backpackers looked angry, as well they might, being lumped in with these more disreputable characters. The rest chose to ignore the whole event, although the Walnut Man, still asleep, moved one hand as though to wipe away the little droplets which fell close to him.

Close to the end of the afternoon the rain stopped or at least slowed down. One by one people began to leave – first the backpackers and then, almost as one group, the other eight.

The last to leave was the white-haired man who had taken quite a long time re-wrapping his books in their protective covering. He stopped by the desk and smiled at us.

"Thank you, all of you," he said, "for your gracious hospitality. We have all appreciated it very much."

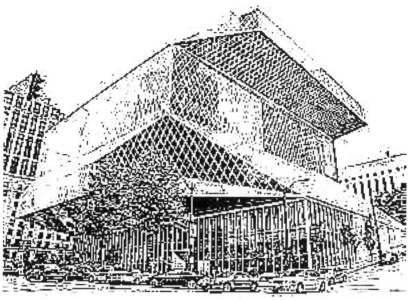

Seattle Public Library – J. Bradley

A Library is the home of the homeless.

G. S. Hilliard 1850

CHAPTER 28 – **THE VAGABOND**

Was he truly a vagabond, a hobo, a vagrant? We never knew his back story, and didn't know if he was homeless, or chose to carry his belongings with him because of some quirk or mental illness, but he was easy to spot as one of his kind.

His many layers of old worn clothing, the long, grayish-white hair and beard, and the skin dark and creased from years in the sun, provided evidence that this man had lived outdoors for many years of his life. His age was indeterminate, and his existence seemed fragile. He had strength, else he would have been unable to carry around the hefty bedroll, two large plastic jugs of water, and other items that were harder to identify. But he did not seem to connect with others on any level. There was the blank stare that indicated lack of desire to engage, and the brisk manner that kept others afar.

How did he find the library? Was there a kind of code shared among those who traveled – like the hobo code of the depression – to indicate that this town was safe and the library offered shelter? We didn't know, but he did find it and visited almost every day it was open. That made us wonder; Where was he when the library was closed? Did he have family nearby, or friends who allowed him to bed down outside or in a shed or barn? How did he eat? He never begged and we saw no fast food wrappers, empty cans or fruit peels. He was very skinny, under the many layers, but he had to eat something. We just never saw what or when.

When he first began coming to the library, there were the usual misgivings. Was he dangerous? Would his odor be so strong as to bother others, including the staff? Would he use the restrooms to clean up? As much as cleanliness was desired, using the public restroom was very problematic, as some homeless tried to pull off a shower using only the sink. We were grateful that he didn't try. He remained a mystery. He came in the winter and stayed until Spring, in the mild weather of our desert community. He was in the library each day arriving soon after opening, and remaining until just before closing. In summer he disappeared, and returned again the following winter. We never knew where he spent the remaining months, if he was near or traveled far, if he moved around or stayed in one safe spot.

His library behavior was only slightly difficult. He never asked to use computers or to checkout books or other items. He did pull large books from the shelves and spent much time with them open on his lap. But the pages didn't move in a regular fashion and he appeared to be studying the words and images with great care. For what, we were never sure. It was difficult to determine if there was a reason for the particular books he chose or if he chose by size, color, or a scheme only he was aware of. Perhaps he had learned that sitting quietly with a book ensured that he would not be bothered by staff. Unfortunately, he tried to return the books to the shelves and the books were usually found in the wrong spot.

Every public library has some characters, and sometimes we know their story. Some have relatives in town, to oversee and keep them fed, or on their medication. Some have told their story to staff members who may offer to help with rides or food.

Others have behavior that makes it obvious that they are just there to sleep, get out of the weather, or follow the voices that drive them. If they are not disruptive or offensive the staff lets them be.

The vagrant was one of these. He was allowed to be, with whatever dignity and character remained in his life.

Cincinnati, OH Library Book Fountain – R. Pendleton

Libraries.....house our dreams

Nikki Giovanni, *American Libraries*, May 1996

CHAPTER 29 - **DALE**

This strange and wonderful branch library has been Let Go by management for several years. Much of my working day is spent trying to impose order on chaos. The patrons watch with interest and sometimes pitch in to help.

Our patron Dale is handicapped and a lobbyist for the local Handicapped organization. He made himself known from practically my first day as Branch Librarian because he walked right into the relatively unprotected staff work room to pick out the new magazines. Then he introduced himself to me and wrote down my name, very businesslike, and asked me to sign a petition in favor of bike paths. Which I did.

I am wary of Dale because our building, an imitation Carnegie style, is absolutely impossible for a handicapped person to get into, and violates about 100 safety ordinances. For example, we have only one exit in case of fire. We are all very nice to Dale, and have planned escape routes to hustle him out at the first whiff of smoke.

Dale is nice to us, too, and hasn't as yet reported us to the ADA folks. He has a different agenda.

For example: the *Los Angeles Times* and the *Bakersfield Californian* are hand-delivered each morning. They used to be thrown on the lawn. Shortly afterward, the automatic sprinklers would go on. So by the time we would get there, the papers would be sopping and had to be spread out over all the available furniture to dry, which means no patrons could sit down until about noon, unless they patted the chair seat first.

So Dale took it upon himself to write the circulation managers of both newspapers and demand that the papers be put into the book drop. The first I heard of his crusade was when both papers called me to apologize. Seems he told them to refer any questions to me.

I was most gracious.

Now Dale comes in daily and puts the dry newspapers on the sticks, which of course gives him first call at reading them and also is extremely helpful to us because we all hate that job.

He next tackles the Book Drop Issue. We have a big one, out by the curb, but the curb isn't marked, so frequently cars park there for a long time, blocking book drop access.

So Good old Dale calls the Street Department and asks, again unbeknownst to me, for the curb to be painted red. Next thing I know a couple of people from the Street Department are out front measuring things, but not carrying any red paint.

Seems that the book drop blocks wheelchair access along the sidewalk -- if somebody in a wheelchair wanted to roll down Baker Street they would have to go on the grass to get around the book drop. So the Street Department wants to cement in some of our grass! Which would be extremely ugly.

I know our front lamp bulbs have long since disappeared and the flag pole has been empty for as long as anybody can remember. But we will defend our grass!

But now they think they want to move the book drop, which I don't want because it will be farther from the building and out of line of sight and much more available for people to crop cherry bombs and ice cream cones into.

But the question is: Shouldn't I be in charge of my own library turf? Also, if I were in a wheelchair, would I mind going on the grass in it? If Dale wants to be in charge, why does he always give the authorities my name and phone number? Why do they take his word that he's been authorized to call?

I don't know but, alas, I do know this: our library has been declared a State Historic Landmark. This of course means it will close and house a special collection.

I don't believe for a moment that this will deter Dale from taking it over.

SECTION 7:

SPECIAL LIBRARY TYPES

Little Free Library Ridgecrest, CA - K. Ray

Had I the power I would scatter libraries over the whole land, as a sower sows his wheat field.

Horace Mann

CHAPTER 30 – **MINI-LIBRARIES**

Libraries come in all sizes, large like the Vatican Library or Library of Congress or tiny like one shelf in a hut. The large ones earn our admiration, but even the small ones entrance us and bring us a joy of discovery. There is a growing trend for small neighborhood libraries on the mini scale which has been the subject of many recent news stories from *American Profile* to the *Los Angeles Times*. These little libraries fill in the gaps for those who find travel difficult or expensive and those who are socially isolated.

The usual mini library is tiny, and is housed in a wooden box or covered shelf. It operates on the simple principle of take one and leave one. Some are well built and painted or crafted into barns, cabins, trains, and other interesting shapes. They are only censored or controlled by the users. Some separate children's from adult books, yet few experience problems of graffiti, theft or damage. No charges for borrowing, or late fees are incurred. There is no policing and rarely are policies needed.

There is one organization, Little Free Libraries - littlefreelibrary.org ,that provides appropriate guidelines and blueprints. They encourage registration and a fee which includes a sign and number. The organization was founded in 2009 by Ted Bol to honor his book-loving mother. He hoped to meet Andrew Carnegie's approximately 2500 libraries and in 2013 it appears that this happened with almost 6,000 in over 36 countries. They assume over 1 million books were borrowed in 2012 and about five to 10 million visitors checked out the libraries. The organization's goals include encouraging literacy and love of reading, and building community.

These libraries have their own discoveries to share. As a visitor looks in the box, he or she finds something. Fiction readers might find a book on birds; a history buff might find a book of poetry. Some readers include notes and reviews of the books inside, others try not to make any marks. Each individual embarks on their own special adventure as they select a book. Instead of finding the small collection an obstacle, it is viewed as a challenge – to locate some book still worthy of one's time. Serendipity rules here.

The articles written about these library "visits" often

highlight the younger and the older visitors. Seniors and schoolchildren are often the walkers in neighborhoods and are first to discover the new libraries. They need no help or special permission to visit or select an item. Unlike restricted parts of their lives, library visits are entirely their own choice. That freedom is very welcome. These two groups are often the most avid and faithful library visitors.

Many libraries have evolved with similar structure and design despite not becoming members of the Little Free Libraries. Perhaps they saw a mini-library someplace and decided to copy the idea or heard of the concept but were unaware of the Little Free Library's existence. Children and seniors are often advocates for the reasons given above. Today, when many individuals feel the stress of everyday life, it is refreshing to be able to find a reason to leave it behind and take a little walk to a kinder, gentler locale. The appeal is broad and the welcome mat is out for the tiny libraries and their patrons.

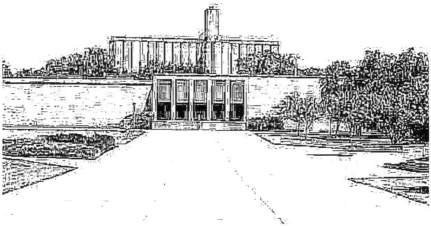

Eisenhower Library, Abilene, KS – R. Pendleton

Don't join the book burners. Don't think you are going to conceal faults by concealing evidence that they ever existed. Don't be afraid to go in your library and read every book, as long as that document does not offend our own ideas of decency. That should be the only censorship.

President Dwight D. Eisenhower

CHAPTER 31 - **PRESIDENTIAL LIBRARIES**

I was thrilled to when the George W. Bush Library opened May 1, 2013. I may not have been thrilled during his presidency, but a library is something we can all enjoy. The library is actually part of an entire

Bush complex located on the campus of Southern Methodist University in Texas. It offers larger than life statues of father and son George Bush, a replica oval office, rose garden, and artifacts such as the megaphone he used at ground zero. It was described in the *LA Times* as "blunt" architecturally, much like the president himself.

Presidential Libraries are some of those little gifts in life that we are delighted to discover and share. More than just libraries they are usually archives, museums and some, burial grounds. They offer wonders to tourists and casual observers as well as serious scholars and historians. If you are fortunate enough to live near one, you are probably aware that they house a wide variety of papers and memorabilia from the president's term. You can view gifts from distinguished visitors, listen to tapes and recordings, read letters and documents and immerse yourself in the trappings of office.

The National Archives and Records Administration, or NARA, operates the thirteen modern presidential libraries from Herbert Hoover through George W. Bush. The eight privately operated libraries are each run by separate federal, state, or private groups. Those include George Washington, John Quincy Adams, Abraham Lincoln, Ulysses S. Grant, Rutherford B. Hayes, William McKinley, Woodrow Wilson, and

Calvin Coolidge.

The very randomness of the libraries seems strange. Some major figures seem to have been overlooked, while minor ones have a library. Why not a Thomas Jefferson, Andrew Johnson, or Theodore Roosevelt Library? We could have a lot of fun with James Madison, James Monroe, or Warren G. Harding and his Teapot Dome scandal. But unlike the modern presidential libraries, these gentlemen did not have the ability to provide input into the location, style, and holdings of their library.

We are fortunate for the generosity of the presidents and their families who provided so much to engage the visitors. As a result, they gain insight into the men who held the office. Harry S. Truman lined his office walls with many of the editorial cartoons that lambasted him during his term. What a treat to see the original signed copies from his critics -- some of whom later came to appreciate him and his sense of humor.

Visitors to John F. Kennedy's library at the University of Massachusetts are treated to beautiful bay views and the lovely little craft that Kennedy sailed there. In Lyndon Johnson's library at the University of Texas in Austin, films document his negotiations ensuring that his Lady Bird got her beautiful highways. Nixon's library was once a battleground, but is quieter today.

The Ronald Reagan Library memorializes the destruction of the Berlin Wall. Early visitors could buy a souvenir piece of "The Wall." It is almost impossible to find a picture of his first wife, Jane Wyman, the mother of his older two children, John and Maureen, perhaps because it was his second wife, Nancy, who was a primary planner.

The Eisenhower Library is housed on grounds that include his childhood home, burial grounds, museum, a statue, memorial, a meditation place (which makes a lovely little chapel), and the always-present gift shop. The tourist can choose from a wide variety of "I Like Ike" buttons and bumper stickers, and a few that like both Ike and Harry (Truman). That interesting marriage of moderate Republican and Democrat is unlikely to happen today. But what a pair they might have made.

The Presidential Libraries provide a more intimate view of the individuals' lives and help us understand their place in history. It is hard not to appreciate the men who served as our presidents whether or not we shared their political views. Their personal papers and their own words give us much richer pictures of these men. These libraries are truly American treasures.

Edmonton, NB, Public Library – R. Pendleton

I am not a crook.
Richard M. Nixon

CHAPTER 32 - **NIXON**

When your library is located in the home town of an American President, you can find yourself in the middle of a Historic Event. That's what happened to me on my first library job. Richard Nixon was born in Yorba Linda, California, where his parents owned a grocery store. A Quaker, he received his undergraduate degree from Whittier College, a small private college known for its Quaker heritage.

The City of Whittier was excited to be the city recognized as the hometown of the President, and when he won reelection handily in 1972, the city was bursting with pride, despite the fact that his only real connection was the time he spent as a student first at Whittier High School and then at Whittier College. Whittier Public Library, as part of the city government, was bursting with civic pride as well, renaming the conference room the Nixon Room.

We hoped the President would come to Whittier Library sometime and sign the new guestbook purchased especially for him. A trophy case in the conference room held photos and other memorabilia which found their way to the library upon his first-term election.

As reference librarians, we were more interested in adding to our reference files than in the various civic happenings. We knew that every high school student would sooner or later write a Nixon term paper, and we worked hard on assembling material about the city itself because tourists were beginning to visit various Nixon-related buildings.

In those days the Internet was not even predicted, and we had no computers of any kind in the library. Instead, we had microfilm readers and photocopiers. We also had drawer upon drawer upon drawer of clippings, letters and other ephemera, and the only still-existing copies of our local newspaper, the *Whittier Daily News.*

Imagine our surprise when we began to receive phone calls, letters, and visits from journalists representing both local papers and some of the major nationally known ones. The Watergate break-in was about to become news, but even before that happened enterprising journalists came looking for articles concerning his youth, his marriage, and his early political career. It was shocking to us to realize that we had, in some cases, the only reports of speeches, hearings, and political campaigns; he was a controversial politician from the very beginning of his career, even when the issues were purely local.

We gradually became used to the fact that our three microfilm readers, ordinarily used for reading old census records for genealogical purposes, were now in use from opening to closing time. We became expert at reading over the reporters' shoulders, to learn for the first time about people and events which would later be big news.

By the time the Watergate scandal broke, even our conference room, the newly named Nixon Room, became controversial, because a local group wanted the library to display anti-Nixon materials, for "equal treatment". This effort peaked during the impeachment trial, but the materials were so readily available by that time that we left the display case as it had been.

With the President's resignation, things returned to normal in the library. He and his wife settled in Orange County, a couple of hours south of Whittier, and never did come to the library. However, several members of the Friends of the Library, who had known and loved Pat Nixon ever since her school teaching days, quietly organized themselves into a support group, sending several members to the Nixon home almost every day, to garden with her and keep her company in her difficult times.

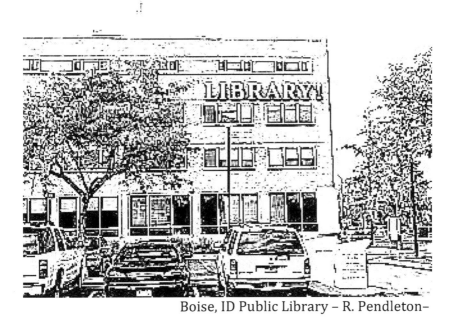

Boise, ID Public Library – R. Pendleton–

Books are lighthouses erected in the great sea of time.

Edwin P. Whipple

CHAPTER 33 - **DISCO**

Deep Springs College, a two-year all-male college on a working ranch between Dyer, Nevada and Big Pine, California, has an interesting and well-used library. Students at Deep Springs are on their way to Ivy League universities and spend their days reading and studying the classics in the mornings and building fences, branding cattle, milking cows, and running the college in the afternoons and evenings. I worked at their library for a couple of years, visiting one day per week to process donations and keep things orderly.

Each time I arrived I would discover something new in the stacks: abandoned shoes, scraps of poetry, hard hats, cups, plates. Some students practically lived in the library. The funniest thing I encountered was the lower half of a mannequin, propped up against one of the windows in the book stacks. It was draped with a string of tinsel. Perplexed, I asked one of the students why it was there. He replied that they had had a disco dance the night before in the library. The entire student body had danced the night away in their beloved library, which they had decorated with magical objects.

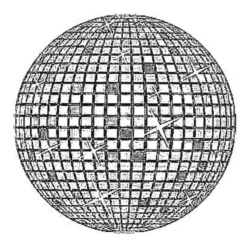

Mt. Carroll, IL, Public Library – R. Pendleton

Perhaps no place in any community is so totally democratic as the town library. The only entrance requirement is interest.

Lady Bird Johnson

CHAPTER 34 - **CARNEGIE**

Librarians are greatly indebted to Andrew Carnegie. The Scot with the penchant for making money was generous in his donations to libraries. In fact he is credited with the founding of over 1600 libraries in the United States, and many others globally. His two tenets, in reading as education, and in sharing his fortune – he believed to die rich would be disgraceful – helped libraries in the United States tremendously. By funding library buildings he contributed to the growth of literacy and learning at a time when school was a luxury few could afford.

Like Bill Gates, Carnegie was one of the richest men in the world during his time. His philanthropy began with the construction of a library in his hometown of Dunfermline Scotland in 1883 and grew into a major effort in the US. His first US Library was built in Pittsburgh in 1890 when there were just over 600 public libraries in the US. He continued building until his death in 1919 when the number of public libraries in the US topped 3500. That era of growth in libraries included the development of the profession of librarianship and the founding of new schools for library science. It was a golden age for both libraries and librarians.

Carnegie libraries were more than just book repositories. Many included auditoriums or were housed with halls or theaters for social, civic, arts, and entertainment events. Carnegie libraries were often designed to support public programs, and serve a variety of community purposes in addition to lending books. To complete the package, the architecture was structurally pleasing. Today many of these libraries have been listed on the register of historic buildings. The majority still serve their publics as places to borrow books and while others have taken new roles as museums, historic sites, etc.

Since Carnegie believed that people should be self reliant he proposed that towns formally request his grants. They had to demonstrate the need for a public library; provide the building site; agree to financially support the library once it was built and finally, agree to provide service free to all. This process was very successful, and is similar to the model used by many nonprofit organizations today. One example is Habitat for Humanity that requires recipients of the houses they build to participate in the building process and thus become invested in the success.

There is a recognizable look to many Carnegie libraries. Whenever one sees a rectangular brick, one or two story, symmetrical library which looks to have been built approximately 100 years ago, chances are good that it is a Carnegie Library. Often located in the central or civic governmental section of a town, the library is still a destination for many people. Most people recognize the building as a comfortable place to visit and spend time.

We can't imagine what our public libraries of today would be like without the Carnegie program. It formed the basis of many large city library systems, including Pittsburgh and New York. Many smaller, isolated areas might still remain unserved without it. To call the program a success is an understatement, and neglects its fundamental goal to help everyone who wanted to read, learn, or gain skills. There is no other individual or program who so fundamentally improved libraries in the United States.

Encino-Tarzana, CA Public Library – J. Christensen

What the world of tomorrow will be like is greatly
dependent on the power of imagination in those who
are learning to read today.

Astrid Lindgren

CHAPTER 35 - **BEHIND BARS**

The Fred C. Nelles School in Whittier was an
institution of the California prison system, housing
boys under the age of 18 who had been convicted of
major crimes. In 1972 I, a newly hired librarian at the
public library, was put in charge of an outreach
program which provided library books to the inmates.

Our plan was to bring a collection of reading materials to the prison once a month and hold a book talk with a selected group of boys. We also consulted on the details of the Nelles library collection. As it turned out, we learned much more than the boys did.

We would drive several boxes of library books to the prison where we would load them onto a book cart. Pushing the cart through the first of several guarded gates was our introduction to this separate world. Inside, we would walk down the corridor to the library, unpack our boxes and set up displays of books. We would present a short program, then turn the boys loose to pick the book or magazine they would keep for the month. Finally we would repack our boxes and make the long walk to the set of gates which would return us to the outside world.

The school was run on principles of behavior modification. The faculty assessed each young man when he entered. They developed a schedule of tasks and goals, assigning each a specific number of points. When he had reached his goal, he would be released, in many cases. In some instances – for example if he had been convicted of homicide – he would remain at Nelles until he turned 18; then he would be transferred to an adult prison. In his case, earning points meant receiving certain benefits within Nelles, such as extra telephone calls.

The behavior modification system was visible throughout the school. For example, although candy was not allowed, students could earn popcorn. The library's major attraction was that it housed a movie-theater-sized popcorn machine which seemed to be continually in use. Students who had earned popcorn points could come in at any time and scoop out a paper bucket of popcorn to take with them.

At first, we tried to entice students to read the books we had brought. I remember we started by showing them a film of the Beatles, and offered several books about them. But these boys professed to know nothing about the Beatles, or even about other rock groups, and in fact disapproved of their long hair (the style for many gangs at the time was short buzz cuts or shaved heads). They thought the film was silly.

Gradually we discovered that almost none of the boys could read. One told me that he had stopped paying attention in school during the second grade. Others made polite efforts to deal with the books, staring at illustrations and turning the pages every now and then. After only a couple of visits we changed to an hour in which we simply read to them. Their favorites were some of the classic children's stories, like Hats For Sale. As for the books, we ended up stocking mostly children's picture books. We had considered using some the graphic novels which were beginning to be published, but the prison had restrictions on what could be read. These restrictions, unsurprisingly, included anything with violence.

The prison library was required by California law to include a legal library. In a separate alcove you could find the California Codes and the standard supplementary materials found in all law libraries. The books were in excellent condition because nobody ever opened them.

We were a popular attraction, because during our visits the boys could be excused from their regular classes if they had earned Library Points. We generally saw the same dozen or so boys, with some new faces each time. One small boy who came each month celebrated his tenth birthday with us (we learned later he was a serial arsonist).

Other popular visitors were the Foster Grandparents. They were a spritely and loyal group, each of whom "adopted" one boy. They taught the boys to knit, and during the time we visited the school a growing number showed up in beanies they had made for themselves. This was the beginning of the awareness of Crips and Bloods, so beanies could not be made in red or blue. We were startled to see large scowling mean-looking young men sporting pastel hats.

Of course, knitting needles could become weapons, so

they were issued by the Foster Grandparent at the start of each visit and returned at the end. I wish I could remember how that affected the knitting, but I don't think it occurred to me to ask then.

The other thing that could be a weapon was something typically found in a library of that time: each card catalog drawer customarily had a spindle which ran the length of the drawer and held the cards. In our case the spindles had been removed, and the threat of somebody tipping over a drawer was always present.

Our outreach project ended after a year for the saddest of reasons: the funding ran out.

Today the Nelles School is deserted, having declared bankruptcy in 2004. The buildings are still there and the grounds are still fenced. The only visitors these days are television crews filming shows like Prison Break.

Main Denver, CO Library – J. Bradley

Librarian Story - We have been told, the first librarian "keeper of books" at Harvard, Solomon Stowell, met the dean walking across the quad one bright day. The dean inquired as to his well-being, and how the library was faring. Stowell replied that all couldn't be better, all the books were safely on the shelves, save one, and he was going to retrieve it right now.

From old Library Lore - but perhaps just a myth

CHAPTER 36 - **IMAGE**
Aka - But you don't look like a librarian

I was watching a recent episode of the TV series *Rookie Blue.* The officers were conducting a sting operation to catch criminals by luring them into a car dealership where they had won a "free car." As two suspects walked into the showroom, two of the officers were assigned to a young male suspect, and the other two officers were told they had "the librarian." Hmm. The "librarian" was a woman, clearly middle aged, small, with straight hair, and dressed in quiet clothes and low-heeled shoes. Even without a bun or cardigan sweater, and no pencils sticking out of her hair or glasses dangling about her neck, she did fit the image. As it turned out, she was not a librarian, simply a widow who failed to manage her finances after her husband died. But the image struck me. Just as we label some women "sluts" for their bright scanty clothing, high heels, overdone make-up and hair, we label other women as librarians for their safe colors, comfortable shoes, and drab appearance.

The image stereotype consists of several elements. First, the librarian is usually a single woman. Just as teachers and nurses have traditionally been female professions, so has that of librarian. The librarian is usually depicted as older, often a spinster who works to support herself, and perhaps lives with her mother. If there is no mother there is usually a cat or two. Eyeglasses are an important part of the image, and are often seen dangling from holders around the neck. The hair is often a bun or short and straight without much style. The woman's clothing is frumpy and often consists of high-necked blouses and long skirts, neither of which are form-fitting, and both of which may be covered by a long cardigan sweater. The blouse or sweater is apt to have a hankie tucked into a sleeve. The outfit tends to end with stockings and dark sensible shoes.

Secondly, the librarian may be seen as unhappy or unfulfilled, since she is single and perhaps even virginal. Not quite a nun, but not socially adept or comfortable with men. Because of this lack in her life, she may be irritable and inflexible, believing in rules and vigilant in her administration of them. She will of course, utter "Shh," to maintain the sanctity of the quiet atmosphere she strives to achieve. She may even guard her patrons from the "dangerous" books with racy passages that might lead them into temptation.

 As a positive, aside from her appearance and her attitude, she is usually assumed to have some intelligence. I love it when a librarian is a contestant on "Jeopardy" because Alex Trebek often comments that they do well on the show. Librarians tend to have a broad range of knowledge and are usually well read. If they are to perform well answering questions, or helping select books, they need to be able to manage a variety of questions, and refer you to many different sources. It's hard to perform these function wells if you are not generally knowledgeable.

The elements of the librarian image or stereotype may vary, but they are predictable enough that even rookie cops know what you mean when you call someone a librarian. I am never sure if I should be insulted by this image. Of course it is not accurate. We know male librarians, young librarians and even "hot" librarians. *Playboy* magazine had an article with scantily clad or unclad librarians to attest that not all are mousy or unfulfilled. We know librarians actually want to keep censorship to a minimum and protect the public's right to read, because it is an important goal of the American Library Association (ALA). We encourage programs for children and adults that bring life and noise into the library. And, sadly, we even know librarians that are ignorant of many books and ideas, who fail at reference questions or advisory services.

So, why does the image persist? Is it good or bad to have such an image?

Stereotypes continue with media support in television, movies, comics, and books despite the valiant efforts of the American Library Association and others to combat them. In television advertising the shushing librarian remains the norm, with her requisite bun and glasses. She is used to advertise candy bars, dictionaries (which seems like a natural), earplugs, laxatives, beer, and energy drinks. Because of the quiet, she has been used in both Saturn and Mercedes Benz ads to attest to the cars' silence. A positive(?) ad campaign was launched by the Wyoming Libraries using a version of the perky truck mud flap silhouette woman reading a book.

One Australian television series, *The Librarians*, featured a public library and the librarians who worked there. The main character, Frances O'Brien, was a very religious and racist head-librarian. Her best friend, Christine Grimwood, was the children's librarian, and other characters were gay, handicapped, and featured other religions and colors. It was a balanced show that exploring the failings of all the characters, and was funny enough to last for three years.

On recent prime time television stereotypical librarians persist in most series, including *Glee, Law and Order*, and *Rookie Blue* to name a few. The interesting television exceptions are both younger male librarians. The Rupert Giles character on *Buffy the Vampire Slayer* is sexy, intelligent, and a helpful mentor to his young students. He is virile and buff and has many women friends and relationships. In the made for television movie, *The Librarian*, the lead character, Flynn Carsen is an over-educated, brilliant adventurer, who nevertheless disappoints his mother because with all his degrees the job he chose was a librarian. Librarians love the heroic character because his knowledge allows him to successfully solve problems.

In cinema, the librarian character has been played by many stars. Mignon Anderson (*A Wife on Trial*, 1917) was poor and alone and married for money as was Barbara Stanwyck who looked for love in *Forbidden*, 1932. Bette Davis was heroic in her attempts to keep a controversial book in *Storm Center*, 1956. Katherine

Hepburn was intelligent and spunky in *Desk Set,* 1957. Shirley Jones, as Marian the Librarian, protected against censorship but remained unfulfilled in *The Music Man,* 1962. Goldie Hawn was resourceful in *Foul Play*, 1978, but Penelope Ann Miller was just silly in *The Gun in Betty Lou's Handbag*, 1992. Rachael Weisz dressed appropriately for the role in *The Mummy*, 1999. Most of these librarians had redeeming characteristics unfortunately many more films perpetuated stereotypes. The shushing, rule-driven, or unhelpful librarian could be found in many films from *Cain and Mabel*, 1936, to *Stanley & Iris,* 1990, and *Billy Elliott,* 2000.

As you would expect, librarians in comics are treated playfully, and often the butt of the joke. It is such a natural subject that most strips have featured the quiet library, the shushing librarian, or the fines for overdue books. Some of the more well known were, *Blondie, Born Loser, Dennis the Menace, Family Circle, Funky Winkerbean, Mother Goose & Grimm, Peanuts*, and *Shoe.* There were a few more positive images of libraries in *Luanne* (She and Gunther volunteer for children's programs), *Nancy*, and *Pricilla's Pop.* Alex Krentzen published an online comic, *Alex...the Librarian,* which featured himself and showed a well-rounded view of the library. In comic books and graphic novels, librarians could be a positive character like *Batgirl* and the detectives Ophelia and

Abbey in the Shirley Damsgaard mystery series.

In books, librarians fare a bit better. According to Christopher Brown-Syed and Charles Barnard Sands in "Librarians in Fiction; a Discussion, (*Education Libraries*. v.21. no. 1, 1997) most are not one dimensional, but are developed characters with positive and negative characteristics.   Many librarians are featured as helpful and kind resources, while others remain the sad, and mousy villains. The most interesting villain is probably Jorge in Umberto Eco's *The Name of the Rose,* who is fiendish and evil. Brown-Syed and Sands also maintain that librarians feature very well in detective fiction. There are many series with librarian detectives including those written by Jo Dereske, Charlaine Harris, Miranda James, Miriam Grace Monfredo, Elizabeth Peters, Ian Samsom, and Judith Van Gieson.

So what are we to conclude from all this, I wonder? The librarian character is alive and is sometimes a stereotype but not always. The stereotype persists because the profession largely supports it. For every youthful librarian who sports bright colors, low necklines, high heels, or fashionable clothing there are two or three older ones who wear muted colors, low heels, high necklines and drab apparel. I once attended a large librarian conference with a friend, who laughingly pointed this out. But we laughed at ourselves as we realized that we too fit the stereotype.

I like to think that librarians care less about appearance because we are focused on ideas, and learning. But I suspect I am just fooling myself. We are human with all the usual foibles, and a few unique ones. As you will (have?) read in these pages, librarians face interesting situations and may or may not respond with grace. I do however, hope you will agree that librarians, and librarianship are not boring.

As to the Harvard Librarian story that begins this section, while I cringe at his attitude, I understand that books were more rare and precious back then, and his protection of them was considered laudable. Under his 16 orders - "No person resident in the College, except an Overseer," and "no Schollar in the College, under a Senior", could borrow a book, and "no one under master of Art (unless it be a fellow) . . . without the allowance of the President." The Harvard Library staff were the only ones entrusted to take books from the shelves. Today, I have the long-range viewpoint of many librarians that having all the books off the shelves and in use was the best. Of course then the collection would be too depleted to be useful, but the empty shelves would prove that the books were well chosen and needed. That is an excellent outcome that most of us would be happy to see.

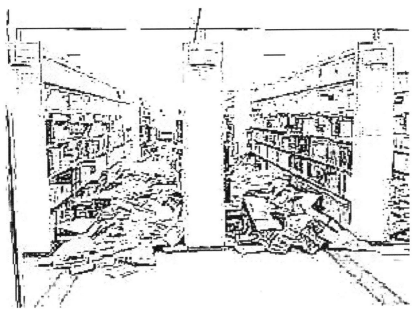

Earthquake damage in Cal State Northridge Library –CSUN.edu

We learn geology the morning after the earthquake.

Ralph Waldo Emerson

CHAPTER 37 - **EARTHQUAKE**

An earthquake is not good for a library. Unfortunately for many parts of the world they are a fact of life. I worked in such a library in Southern California. Our specific area had many earthquakes; in one year we suffered over 100 with a magnitude of 4 or higher. That spurred Sony to make an ad featuring their then new Walkman CD player, which began: "We're in the shakiest city in California..." This is a world where the San Andreas Fault is well known.

Today most libraries in earthquake zones are well-braced, and protected against major damage from book shelves collapsing or falling. Years of earthquake experiences have taught us how to protect against major damage. In the US, state and local regulations, backed by OSHA, insure that necessary precautions are taken. The usual cause of a problem in a library is due to the books themselves falling off the shelves. The shelves may remain upright and firmly attached to the wall, but the books, magazines, signage, and other items may fall. You always hope that no one is hurt.

If you have been in a library during an earthquake you will remember it. There is an eerie feeling when the shelves of books begin to sway back and forth or undulate snake-like. And items begin to fall from shelves. Growing up in California your thoughts usually jump to questions like: "Is this the BIG one?" or "How far are we from the epicenter?" In earthquake areas everyone marks their favorite app or website for information. We used the Cal Tech seismologists who kindly marked each quake with a square using different sizes and colors for intensity and time.

Since most libraries are not open 24 hours, the odds

favor larger quakes happening during hours when the library is closed. That's preferable to having any injuries. Typically the staff returns to work finding a scene of chaos with books in tumbled piles on the floor between the shelves. With a large earthquake, even if its epicenter was many miles away, the result is a big mess.

That was what we found after our major quake. It looked at first glance that most of the books had fallen to the floor. We quickly saw that we had a lot to do. First we had to be sure the library was safe for people. The firemen came and assured us that the building structure, gas, water, and electric services were fine. We had moved to a building with no elevator or stairs, so we didn't need to check them. It took time and expertise beyond my knowledge but the building was eventually judged safe for entry.

We were not as lucky in our annex. The electronic space-saving moveable shelving – a source of pride when working well, had jumped its tracks. Since the remaining shelves were locked closed, we couldn't access the materials. We called the manufacturer who promised to send out a team to assess and repair the shelves. We had to let everyone know that most of the bound volumes were unavailable. The team came and informed us that the shelves would need new parts. It took weeks to order and install. The cost came out of the library budget. Sigh.

Back in the main library we checked each book and assessed if it needed to be repaired, rebound, or scrapped. Sadly, many large volumes fell from one of the top shelves. They had broken bindings or covers, torn pages, and were missing entire sections. Of course we had no additional budget for those repairs either.

We were fortunate when word got out about our tragedy. Many library patrons came to help us. Our users were well-educated and eager to help us – we believed we were fortunate. Most people think they know how to correctly shelve books in Library of Congress, our cataloging system. After our experience, I feel it is safe to say that most people DO NOT know how to accurately shelve books. All the wonderful volunteers assured us they needed no supervision. We learned otherwise, when we had to track down and re-shelve the hundreds of books that they shelved incorrectly.

Over time, we were able to "fix" the earthquake damage, but none of us will ever forget the experience. I only hope we learned some lessons from it, and will be able to do a better job next time. Of course, we hope there never is a next time!

NY Public Library Lion – R. Pendleton

The three most important documents a free society gives are a birth certificate, a passport and a library card.

E. L. Doctorow

CHAPTER 38 – **GOING TO COURT**

Librarians have a variety of duties depending upon their level in the organization. If you supervise staff or budget, your responsibilities are greater than if you are one of the staff who primarily follow orders. In a large county, one supervisor may manage a group of small branch libraries and be responsible for the oversight of their day-to-day activities. My supervisor managed about 6 smaller branches in addition to our own medium sized branch, and I was her replacement if she was ill, on vacation, or just unavailable. The challenge is that you are not present at the small branch and events may occur that you have no personal knowledge of. You must trust the staff who run the smaller branch to do a good job. Sometimes that is hard to do.

One of our small branches had a manager who had been there for a very long time, and had recently lost a child in a mysterious and unsolved murder. She and her staff had the added stress of moving her library to new quarters. The combined stresses impacted her and the branch no longer ran smoothly. There were times when the branch manager reported problems that disappeared when they were investigated. We began to believe that the manager was so stressed that she was unreliable and often missed the facts – she was flaky. She was encouraged to take time off and get some therapy, but work seemed her refuge and she didn't take leave. Nothing improved.

My supervisor had the responsibility of going to small claims court of behalf of the county library system. She did so once every 3-4 months. The goal was to collect fees owed to the library by individuals who had not paid their fines, or had lost books and not reimbursed the county. The fees went into the general county fund. We had always secretly felt that the fees should go to the library so that they could support the book collection, but that wasn't how it worked. My supervisor took me with her once to see the court process. It seemed to work like clockwork. She stood before the judge, told the charges, which there was no one there to rebut, and the judge granted the claim to the county.

My supervisor decided it was time for me to try to go to court – alone. This time the claim was not from our branch, but for the other branch – the one with the flaky manager. The claim was for reimbursement for five books which had been checked out and never returned by the branch. This time, however, the woman who had checked the books out attended the court hearing. She had driven for over an hour and taken time off of work to attend. Her report was that she had returned all of the books, and had even seen one on the shelf later. She came to court to show her son that the judicial system was fair and just. She spoke in an impassioned voice with a slight British accent. Her appearance was professional, and she seemed very clear and organized. She was a reliable witness.

I knew how our branch handled such cases. If a patron reported that a book had been returned we liked to give them the benefit of the doubt. We granted them extra time to search their cars (books were often found under or between seats) and in their homes where the book might sit hidden amidst their own books. We asked patrons to check if they might have possibly returned it to the wrong library, to a school, business, or our local community college. We regularly found books in the book drop from other libraries that we returned to the rightful owners. Meanwhile, our staff scoured the shelves to make sure that the books had not been returned but inadvertently not checked in. Most of the time the patrons found their books. Sometimes we found them on our shelves, and the matter was cleared. In the days before sophisticated computer systems, it was easy to miss checking a book in or out, and the record would wrongly show that the patron still had it.

We tried to be rigorous in resolving such claims and if a case of ours went to court, we had already spent months tracking down every possibility to find the book. That is why patrons didn't fight the court case; they knew they owed the money. This one, however, seemed a very different situation.

I felt sick to my stomach. It was possible that the smaller branch had searched and failed to find the books, but I was doubtful. The flaky manager was not careful with her records or her follow-ups, and I believed this patron. She was positive she had returned the books, and even remembered the date and circumstances. She had seen one of the books she returned on a shelf in the library in the next few weeks. She could have seen a different copy of the book, but that was not likely in a small branch. It was easy for the flaky manager to pass the problem off to us. She did not have to go to court to defend her claim against the patron but now I did.

I listened as the judge questioned the woman, and watched as she presented her side of the story. It was certainly possible that she had failed to return the books. I had seen many patrons, just as sure that they had returned books, sheepishly return with the found items shortly after. But she had pointed out to the branch manager that she believed the books were on the shelf and the manager ignored her, or forgot to follow up. The woman maintained that she did not mind giving money to the library, but she believed she was right and didn't owe the money. I became convinced that she had returned the books as she said. But I had no training in the court and no guidance in what to do – either to drop the case or ask for more time to resolve it. I was supposed to leave court with a resolved claim and funds for the county. I had never seen or heard of another outcome.

I felt worse each minute. I watched the defendant's child who was supposedly learning about democracy and the justice of the court system. If you were right shouldn't you win your case? That was the point she was making on behalf of her son. I agreed with her reasoning. But I still didn't know what to do.

I was relieved, but only temporarily, when the judge told that court, that he would think about the case before he rendered his verdict. Perhaps there was time to remedy the situation. I rushed back to my branch and spoke to the supervisor. She listened as I told her of my fears that the flaky manager hadn't really looked for the lost books, perhaps fearing the supervisor would note it against her. The supervisor didn't know how to change the county point of view at this part of the process. If we had doubts, we should have resolved them prior to the court date, but this one had happened quickly and we had to rely on the other branch to do the right thing. We just weren't sure that they were still capable of doing that.

We eventually sent a note to the judge telling him our concerns. We never heard back directly, but we understood that the judge ruled for the patron not the library. Soon after, the flaky manager took an early retirement and we didn't have another small claims problem with that branch during my library years.

Downtown Elizabeth, IL Library – R. Pendleton

Librarians are almost always very helpful and often almost absurdly knowledgeable. Their skills are probably very underestimated and largely underemployed.

Charles Medawar

CHAPTER 39 - **MAGIC**

This should actually be titled the magician or the pull the rabbit from the hat trick as it refers to the librarian's ability to find "the book" or article the individual patron is seeking with almost no information.

Years ago when I attended library school the prevailing wisdom was that a librarian, especially a reference librarian, needed to have a broad range of knowledge in order to help patrons. This worked for finding books, articles, favorite authors, recordings, movies and sometimes the items left inside the book that were accidentally returned to the library. It helped to know that Sibelius was a composer, Erte was the artist, Leeuwenhoek a scientist, and Citation was a race horse. That information was a starting point for finding books and articles that might be needed for that important school report, to settle the big bet, and it helped to establish your future credentials.

A fun adjunct of the magic was helping to find books similar to books the patron already knew and liked. It was good to know that a child who liked Judy Blume would also probably like to read Paula Danziger, and Norma Fox Mazer. Today you would find followers of Harry Potter books by authors Ursula LeGuin, C. S. Lewis, and J.R. R. Tolkien. We'd find authors like Van

Velde and Anderson to keep the Stephanie Meyer's *Twilight* series lovers happy. If patrons liked Sue Grafton mysteries, we'd steer them to Nevada Barr, Sarah Paretsky, and Dana Stabenow. Most readers of John Grisham would also enjoy books by Phillip Friedman, John Lescroart, and Scott Turow.

Ultimately, as we've seen by the articles on reference questions, the librarian must use some ingenuity to help the patrons. In one excerpt from his book *Mountains beyond Mountains*, James Farmer shares his experience with such a request - paraphrased here:

The parents of some fellow students owned a bookstore. They gave James a copy of J.R.R. Tolkien's trilogy, *The Lord of the Rings*. He read it all in a couple of days – then read it again. He brought the book to the library and told the woman at the desk, "I want other books like this." She gave him a handful of fantasy novels. He brought them back. "No, this isn't it." This went on for a time, until she finally handed him *War and Peace*. "This is it." He told the librarian. "This is just like *The Lord of the Rings*." He was eleven, but she had learned not to underestimate her readers.

Many such experiences were not so successful. Taking my ninth grade English class to the library to select a book was a nice experience for most students. One came up to me, and earnestly asked for a title of a book that changed the world. I suggested Darwin's, *The Origin of the Species*. As her face fell, I understood my mistake. We were in South Carolina and she was a good Baptist creationist. I quickly added some other titles for her to choose from, but she never again asked for my advice.

The reader's advisory function described above, in knowing authors and similar works has been carried out professionally by the likes of Nancy Pearl and other librarians who read so widely, that they are able to recommend books on almost every subject. The books *Now Read This, Book Lust,* and Nancy's blog offer great selections. (Nancy's other major distinction was having a librarian action figure designed in her image, complete with a moveable hand for shushing.)

Reader's advisory, however, does not have the same magical impact of being able to identify a book by its cover or even its color. Yes, librarians can do that. At a recent meeting of librarian friends we talked about some tricks employed for just that. One librarian looked up the cover art and illustrations that accompanied book purchase sites (think Amazon & Barnes & Noble) to find books when the patron could only describe the picture on the cover.

An even more spectacular feat was reported by a librarian whose entire collection had been moved.

She diagrammed the location of each shelf from the old location and where it was now found in the new building. And yes, patrons did come in to ask where the long set of green books on the lowest shelf had moved and were pleased that the librarian knew the exact location.

This "finding" of books by their physical features vice their authors, titles, and dates, is what may set librarians, and talented bookstore staff, apart from the masses. Many library goers may be unable to remember the name of the dictionary they use, but they will remember it as the big red book on the stand by the drinking fountain.

That simple description will allow most librarians to locate it. It's a trick that serves to help regular library-goers who use the library often, but not very well.

Today, some of the same skills will work, even if the item is searched via Google, or a specialized database vice a card catalog, or the librarian's memory. If you don't know how to spell or can't remember who is who, or what's what, you can't know if you are even close to the answer the patron is seeking.

Librarians love to create that magic, and pull that bunny from the hat. But for them, it's just part of the job.

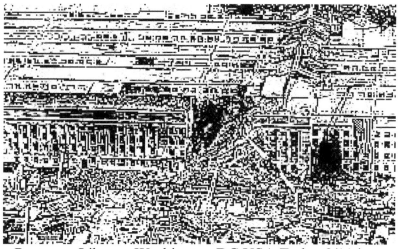

Pentagon Library, Washington DC USA Today 9/11 image

Today as never before, the fates of men are so intimately linked to one another that a disaster for one is a disaster for everybody

Natalia Ginzburg

CHAPTER 40 - **NINE-ELEVEN**

WHANGDEPOOTENAWAH, is the Ojibwa word for disaster; an unexpected affliction that strikes hard. It seems an apt description of the 9-11 attack and its aftermath.

We all live someplace, and each place has its own special problems. If you live in the Southeast, you are aware of the hurricanes. Northerners and Easterners are familiar with harsh blizzards, rain, and flooding.

Midwesterners must deal with tornadoes. On the West Coast, earthquakes are the norm. And every place with paper, film, and other combustible materials must deal with the potential for fire.

Libraries are as prone to damage as their surroundings and every natural – and man-made disaster brings its toll. Clean-up, repair, and replacement are all part of library work, and everyone prays that they avoid major problems. But like life itself, library work has ups and downs, and disasters are part of the story. One major dramatic example occurred September 11, 2001.

Military librarians were especially aware of the attack on the Pentagon, the damage to the Pentagon Library and the experience of Ann Parham, the Librarian of the Army. Like many other Pentagon, and 9/11 survivors, Ann was shocked and injured during the attack. She had watched some of the events transpiring in New York, and as others, had concerns about the Pentagon, but did not have information that was specific enough to warn her that she should leave. She continued her regular duties, and was returning to her desk after sending a fax, when the attack began.

According to the report by the Historical Office with the Office of Secretary of Defense, "The heat was suffocating and the smoke-filled air so dense that Ann 'felt like I was in London...and that this was a very foggy...night.'...The fireball caused flash burns on her face and hands, her eyes were burning, and a flaming ceiling tile burned off a two-inch swath of hair." She was coated with Jet A, a dangerous, smelly, very flammable liquid fuel and suffered lacerations and a broken toe. After she was helped out and arrived at the hospital, she realized that her plastic Pentagon identification badge had curled from the heat of the fire.

Per Richard Cooper in the *Los Angeles Times*, the only thing that separated Ann from the E-Ring where the plane hit was the copy machine room. The LA Times story indicates that the fireball apparently swept over her from behind. Something crashed down from the ceiling and hit her head. "As she limped blindly through smoke and debris, smelling her burnt hair, feeling the pain from her peeling skin and a blow that had momentarily knocked her to the floor, Ann Parham thought about her mother." She thought about the kind of news her mother would be getting. "I didn't want that to happen, so I kept moving." Ann told the reporter, "It's the most horrific thing I've ever gone through. I hope I never have to go through anything like it again." She related. "I am very, very fortunate. I am blessed. Other people, I'm afraid, were not so fortunate."

Prior to the attack on 11 September, the Pentagon

Library was scheduled to move into a new space within the Pentagon, designed specifically for the library. As a result of the damage, space in the Pentagon was at a premium, so the new library space was reassigned to another Army organization. The library collection (after being treated to minimize the effects of water damage and mold resulting from the fire) and staff were moved out of the Pentagon to a temporary location in the Taylor Building in Crystal City, a 10 minute shuttle bus ride away from the Pentagon.

The Office of the Administrative Assistant to the Secretary of the Army (OAASA) planned to make the library's move out of the Pentagon permanent. The library had been in the Pentagon serving Department of Defense personnel since 1944. The library would not be able to effectively accomplish its mission if it were physically separated from the people it served. It was at this point that Ann began to work with librarians, historians, speech writers, and other library users to persuade the Administrative Assistant (AA) to return the library to the Pentagon.

In 2002, to show a presence in the Pentagon, the library staff set up a table on the Pentagon Concourse where they gave away free books and magazines. Mena Whitmore, Pentagon Library Director, identified a vacant store front on the concourse and was successful in obtaining it for the library later that year. The store front was very popular and heavily used. However, the space was limited so most of the staff and the collections remained in the Taylor Building. Meanwhile, a temporary Butler building, located just outside the Pentagon, was provided for interim use by the library in April 2003. The library remained in this building until the fall of 2006 when it moved to its permanent home within the Pentagon, in the renovated facility which also houses the Pentagon Conference Center. Although a number of people helped Ann accomplish this task, one person, Dr. Alfred Goldberg, Chief, Historical Office, Office of the Secretary of Defense, was instrumental in the return of the library to the Pentagon.

During the entire time period of disaster, cleanup, relocation and rebuilding, the librarians continued to provide library and reference services to Department of Defense personnel. They understood that by "soldiering on" the work they believed in would benefit the country they served.

Today the Pentagon Library remains inside of the Pentagon and is open for regular business, staffed by dedicated military librarians.

Former Wal-Mart - McAllen, TX Library – R. Pendleton

Do not go where the path may leave, go instead where there is no path and leave a trail.

Ralph Waldo Emerson

CHAPTER 41 - **GRAND THEFT**

Librarians have long been stereotyped for their appearance and demeanor. My friends and fellow workers have joked about the "safe colors and sensible shoes" they associate with librarians. Librarians have even made fun of each other, spotting them at conferences and singing out "Bogie at 4 o'clock." My poor mother believed I would be a spinster if I didn't spruce up my plain wardrobe. She implored me to "show a little more," meaning cleavage. Instead I persisted in wearing clothes I liked, including a long dark dress with a lace collar – the one she called my librarian dress. Even the *Playboy* feature on sexy librarians didn't change opinions.

The librarian stereotypical image comes with expected behaviors as well as clothing. The frown and the shushing, the bun and the pencil, the hanky in the sleeve are all part of the expected uniform. So, it should surprise many to know that librarians have been guilty of crimes – in this particular instance, a felony: Grand Theft Auto.

It began innocently enough. A colleague, Susan, and I found that we were compatible travelers. She represented a military library located on the East Coast, and I represented the same entity on the West Coast. We could commiserate about problems with staff or budget and each of us understood the other's concerns. We found that we both liked to try the food, music and drink of cities where we attended library conferences. So we often attended together and networked along the way. It was a good relationship that worked for us both.

This particular meeting was to discuss some library consortia buying plans. It was hosted by a librarian in San Diego, California. I drove to the library, and Susan flew in to the airport and rented a car. We met late at the hotel and discussed our meeting strategy.

The next morning Susan and I met for a quick breakfast and walked to the parking lot. Susan offered to drive and walked up to a small red compact. She clicked the electronic key and the door unlocked. She and I both got in. I noticed a pair of sunglasses and asked Susan if they were hers. She looked and said, no, and guessed that they belonged to the rental agency staff who cleaned the car before she picked it up. The turnover of cars at the airport was rapid and we both understood how someone could leave something in a car. She said she would return the glasses when she brought the car back.

We approached the gate of the base that was the site of our meeting and stopped to complete the necessary paperwork for a car pass. Our host had paved the way for us and it didn't take long. Armed with our pass and our meeting paperwork we met up with the other librarians. After a long day of discussing options and priorities for the consortia buys we ended the meeting at about five o'clock. Our hostess mentioned a lighthouse just a few minutes up the hill that was a worthwhile sight. We could access it since we had a pass. We enjoyed the lighthouse and the views of the Pacific and then returned to the hotel to get ready for the dinner we had planned with our colleagues.

We took my car to the restaurant, and enjoyed a nice evening with good wine, old friends and lively conversation about books, music, movies and television shows. Susan and I again met for breakfast and then went back to our rooms to get ready for our meeting. As I was moving to the door, I got a phone call. It was from the concierge at the front desk, asking if I had been driving the car in the parking lot with the base pass in the window. They saw my name on the pass and assumed that I was the driver. They saw the room registered in my name and called. I told them that I was in the car, but as a passenger. They asked about the driver and I told them. They thanked me and hung up. As I went down to meet Susan I wondered if there was an issue with parking, or if we needed a hotel parking pass? There had been no mention, but maybe we did.

When I met Susan, she was flushed and upset. She pulled me out of the hallway and into her room. The hotel manager had called to ask about the car. He said it belonged to another guest at the hotel and had been missing over 24 hours. He wanted to know how she happened to be driving it. The police were in the lobby and wanted to interrogate us. They had put out an all points bulletin for the missing car and had been looking for it. The guest had been shocked to find "her" car in the parking lot of the same hotel that morning after it had been missing all day yesterday.

After a long discussion with the police and hotel management, Susan was allowed to leave, but cautioned that they might still need us for questioning later. She found out that the car we took the day before was not her rental at all, but belonged to another guest. When we went to the parking lot, we found Susan's car about six cars farther down the line past the one with the parking pass we had driven the day before. Her electronic key opened both cars! The cars were very similar in size, color and appearance. One was a Dodge, the other was a Plymouth, and both were Chrysler Motors products.

We went to the lobby to explain the mix-up with the hotel management, and were very chagrined to find the real owner of the car there too. We waited until she had finished her tirade against the hotel and we felt terrible because we knew the hotel was not to blame. Who knew that car keys were interchangeable? We had no idea. Now we know that a manufacturer issues the same key approximately once out of every 10,000 keys. They strive to keep them with different models and different destinations, but they can't control everything. Since people know their own car and its unique markings, it isn't considered a major problem. Only in rare cases such as ours, is there an issue. Rental cars aren't unique, and people rarely check the license if the door key works. We are certainly more careful now, but we never thought that one key could open other doors.

As we told the hotel manager more, he shared the details of the other guest's anger. She had been an instructor hired to teach a course in the city. She had all of her materials in the trunk of her car. She hadn't brought them inside the hotel because they were safe in the trunk, and she would just drive them to the class the next morning. But as we now know, when she went to her car the next morning the car was gone with all of her materials inside. She used her car key to double check the license number, but her car was not there. She contacted the hotel management and they helped her call the police and file a stolen car report. Because of the proximity to the Mexican border and the added value of the educational materials in the trunk, the theft was considered a high priority. After hearing the instructor in the lobby, we understood the police; she was irate and very dominating and loud, but we understood her unhappiness. We thought about apologizing, but having seen her anger, we didn't think she would accept that, so we kept quiet.

We arrived late at our meeting and had to tell the story to everyone. We were still worried that the police might be after us, but no one called or came to arrest us. We were very cautious about going back to the hotel and tried to avoid the lobby or the parking lot when we saw the "other car. We ignored all the funny looks and pointing by the hotel staff and tried to avoid the public areas. We left the next day after successfully agreeing on our consortia purchases with the other librarians.

We weren't sorry to leave, but we never lived down our reputations as car thieves with the other librarians.

Section 9

REFERENCE WORK

Little River, NZ Science Centre & Library – J. Bradley

Librarians, Dusty, possess a vast store of politeness. These are people who get asked regularly the dumbest questions on God's green earth. These people tolerate every kind of crank and eccentric and mouth-breather there is.

Garrison Keillor

CHAPTER 42- **QUESTIONS**

Understanding what someone is asking is the art of reference service, and is why the reference interview is so important. Much like a doctor taking a patient's history, asking someone why they want information and how they will use it is critical to finding the right answer. Unfortunately, it is often difficult to tread between personal and private information in order to find out what the library patron really hopes to find. It is just as true today where much of what we find for patrons is online as it was in the past when we could only find information in books. If someone is having problems in their work, financial, health or personal life, helping them may be critical to their well-being. Finding a resource for dealing with bankruptcy, divorce, depression or domestic violence is satisfying to the librarian but also brings with it a certain angst.

On the lighter side is just helping to find a trivia answer, or resolving a minor dispute. Who had the better lifetime batting average?, or What is the longest river? The answers may change over time so having current information is very important. Most librarians have a memory of at least one time when they answered a question that brought a true sense of satisfaction. My question came in a public library early in my career, where the most important questions I had answered up until then consisted of, What was Cary Grant's real name? Archibald Leach - which earned a free hamburger at a fast food restaurant, or What other foods besides spinach are high in iron? - for an anemic woman.

Two teenage girls brought me my question. They looked about 15. One was quiet and seemed rather nervous. The other did most of the talking. She approached me and said, "My friend wants a book on hygiene." That seemed a rather old-fashioned term for these two youngsters, and it was a little puzzling to me. I suspected that they were using hygiene as a euphemism for the female reproductive system. Years or perhaps generations earlier, "hygiene" classes were used to introduce youngsters to the topic of sex on a very basic level.

I wanted to be sure I wasn't assuming too much, and didn't want to offend them. I also wasn't sure what level of information they needed. It was tricky because they were old enough to seek out answers without their parents, but were they capable of understanding clinical medical information? Was that what they wanted? This went through my head quickly as I began to formulate a question for them. "Would you like some information on female health?" The speaker nodded her head yes, but the other girl just looked at the floor. I made a decision and took them to the children's section where there were some basic and mid-level books that wouldn't offend anyone if they were taken home. But on the way there I wondered if that would be the right answer. I pulled two or three books from the shelf and opened them up to show some of the words and illustrations. The speaker smiled to show that I was on the right track, but the other girl looked at them a bit and finally spoke. "I think we need more." This was hopeful because it showed we were on the right track. Because they were teens it was appropriate to step up the response, and I said, "Then we should go to the adult section." They both looked a little happier, so I felt I was approaching an answer.

We reached the adult nonfiction medical area and I showed them some of the titles. "This is where you can find some information that might be able to help." At least I hoped so. They said thank you and began to browse through the books. I wondered if the issue was pregnancy or STD. I hoped not for their sake, but knew that at least they could find answers in the books. I was busy with other patrons for a while but could see the girls looking through the books for the next 20 to 30 minutes. Then, the speaker caught my eye and waved me over. Her friend looked even more miserable. The speaker looked at me and said, "We haven't really found what we were looking for." Hmm, they had spent enough time in the books to find out a lot, so I wasn't quite sure what they might need. "What would you like to find?" I asked. The speaker took a deep breath and said, "My girlfriend's boyfriend wants to have sex, but she isn't ready. Do you have something we can show him?"

I thought, then said, "You'd like some arguments to present to him to explain why you should wait." They both smiled and nodded their heads. I couldn't think of any books that did more than offer statistics on the dangers of disease or pregnancy. But I did remember some pamphlets that had been put out by Abigail Van Buren – *Dear Abby* – that had addressed this very problem. We had a pamphlet file, so that was our next stop. I wished we had had the exact pamphlet, but it wasn't there. But we did come up with a list of pros and cons that we could use. The only pro was the satisfaction of the young man, the cons were many and the girls both seemed very relived.

I hoped that armed with the information they would be comfortable dealing with the problem. I was very appreciative that the friend was so helpful in making sure we really addressed the actual question. If she hadn't been there to tell, translate and give clues we might have been stuck in the Hospital practices area. Instead I felt good that day believing I had probably helped someone.

Nauvoo, IL Public Library – R. Pendleton

Google can bring you back 100,000 answers, a librarian can bring you back the right one.

Neil Gaiman

CHAPTER 43 - BEAUTIFUL?

Shortly after I became a reference librarian, McDonald's ran a hugely popular contest involving answers to questions on many topics, from word definitions to geography to historical events. Much of our time at the reference desk was devoted to fielding phone calls from people eager to win a McDonald's prize.

One late afternoon I picked up the phone to hear a man's voice ask, "what is the definition of callipygian?" I had no idea, so I obediently trotted over to the nearest unabridged dictionary and brought it to the phone. Then I started to read the definition: "Having beautifully proportioned buttocks."

At this point I could hear more voices in the background. The gentleman quickly said, "Thanks" and hung up. I looked around the room to see whether anybody had overheard me, but all of our patrons were studiously involved in their reading.

In just a few minutes the phone rang again. It was the same man. "I'm sorry if I embarrassed you," he said. "My friend thought it would be funny to call the library and make them read it. I told him I thought it was a bad idea."

Apparently it was not a McDonald's question after all, but more like some of the bar bets we would get from time to time. But I have never forgotten that particular definition.

History

After spending a long morning viewing videotapes of famous people's speeches, the young man sighed and said what he really needed was a videotape of Abraham Lincoln giving his Gettysburg Address speech. When I explained there was no videotape back then, he said an audio would be OK. I had to explain there was no electricity back then, so there was no technology available to record, other than paper, what was said. Two years later, when I had to attend the graduation ceremonies as faculty, that young man marched and received his diploma with a major in history. All true and the name and location of the college will remain undisclosed.

More History

A second favorite story was a woman who dashed in, looking just like a mother who needed a book for her son's book report THAT MINUTE.

"I need a photo of Shakespeare as a teenager."

"But we don't have any photos like that." It was definitely the wrong answer.

"If you don't have that, I guess I'll just have to settle for a photo of him as an adult."

Quickies?

I have some reference questions which will be my favorites forever. The first one was presented to me on the very first evening I was on the reference desk. It came from a well-dressed middle-aged woman who pretty clearly had come directly from her office to the library in search of just the right information. I hoped to impress her with my knowledge, plus my efficiency, but it didn't work that way, because it took so long for me to understand her question.

"I want a book of brief cases."

Well, we discussed whether magazines would be more appropriate than books (I was thinking about catalogs of luggage), then we browsed in travel guides (she looked extremely mystified here, but was polite). Finally I stopped dashing here and there, and began to ask her more pointed questions. Somewhat exasperated, she said slowly, "Brief. Cases."

And finally she said, "Like Reader's Digest."

The light dawned. She wanted anecdotes of funny or weird stories about trials and court appearances. The cases were found for the patron.

***

And there was the patron who wanted information about the "Sucks" Indians. A book on the Sioux Indians worked just fine.

Unflappable

I had worked in academic Libraries exclusively for years before getting a job as a Librarian at Oakland Public Library. I worked at one of the busiest desks at the very busy Main branch in downtown Oakland. One of the veteran librarians who trained me commented on the varied and sometimes strange reference questions that people would ask – all very different than the types of questions asked by students at academic libraries. One of the ones she shared with me that has always made me chuckle is "Do cockroaches f**k?"

Any reference question is taken seriously by librarians, even ones that seem shocking and crude. Patrons from all walks of life are treated with respect. After consulting the best resource, it was found that cockroaches do, indeed, have intercourse. They mate facing away from each other with their genitalia in contact, and copulation can be prolonged. One more library user was linked to crucial information by a studious and unflappable librarian.

Saint Somebody

A middle-aged chubby woman in a blue dress came in just after lunch.

She: "Do you have a book on Ann?"

Me: "??????"

She: "Well, maybe it is Saint Ann. I couldn't find it at the other library. They didn't know what I was talking about (flounce)."

Me: "Is that the title of the book? Are you looking for information about a particular saint?"

She: "I don't think she was a saint."

Me: "Do you think Saint Ann is the name of a book? Is this a true story, or a novel?"

She: "It's for my daughter."

Me (getting desperate): "How old is your daughter?"

Pause.

She: "She is in tenth grade."

Ok. Not missions, not state reports, maybe not biography book report. Probably not the science fair required project.

Me: "So you are looking for Ann. Do you remember if Ann has a last name?

She: "Now that I think about it, it's probably Saint somebody but not Ann."

[Have you all got it yet? I hadn't.]

Me: "What class is this book for?"

She: "English class."

A-HAH!!

Me: "There's a play by George Bernard Shaw called *Saint Joan*. Do you think it could be that play?"

She: "Now why didn't the other library tell me that?"

P.S. We found the play. Of course, it still could be something completely else.

Littlest Library (unknown location) – R. Pendleton

The next best thing to knowing something is knowing where to find it

Samuel Johnson

CHAPTER 44 - **SATISFACTION**

Much of any work is drudgery that we must move past in order to get to that part of the job that we enjoy. We can't always predict when the unusual or interesting parts will appear to break up the day or bring the satisfaction that we need to keep us motivated and productive – at whatever task we choose. In the library world, that good feeling doesn't come every day and is sometimes a rare occurrence. So, when an opportunity arrives to achieve that special sense of satisfaction, we are sure to remember it.

My favorite memory of a satisfying event came while working in a military library on a base that supported new and innovative technology as well as standard operations. The operations at that time were chiefly in Iraq for the conflicts that took place in the early part of this century. This was not long after September 11, 2001 and we all knew soldiers, sailors, and marines who were currently deployed, and many of their family members who remained behind.

Our library role was primarily to support the scientists and engineers working on the base, but we helped others with interlibrary loans, reference, and other requests which fell into our purview. We also provided real-time response to a group that interfaced with the troops daily. We rarely interfaced with actual troops, but were happy knowing that we were doing what we could to help.

It was during the holidays, after Christmas but before New Years and the base was almost deserted as most people took the time off to visit family, use up end-of-year vacation days, and unwind. The library staff was about one-third of the usual, and the patrons were fewer than that. We received a phone call from an air tech support crew in Iraq. He had military access and therefore, saw the library on the base Intranet, and decided that we might have the manual he needed. His job was to install new equipment on a fleet of aircraft, and he had been sent the equipment but not the manual on how to accomplish this feat.

He tried the folks who sent the equipment, but they didn't have the manuals. He tried the manufacturer – closed for the holidays. He tried other numbers he thought might work, but no one answered, until he called the library. The library staff recognized the importance of getting the aircraft off the ground and back into service. They knew that planes stuck on the ground were targets, and of no help to the troops who might need close air support. So the library searched, and called, and called back and checked with the people who should have the manual.

The developers of the necessary manual had an electronic copy that would work if only they could email it. But the current email system couldn't support such a large file. The library staff needed to find another way to get it out. So, again they searched and called and searched some more. They then learned of other specialized email systems used to work with the troops. They investigated, and tried, and failed, but didn't give up. They continued to try every avenue available to them, not once, but as many times as it took. And finally they were able to email the manual to the air crew. The crewman was so happy he sent everyone a long thankful email. His Christmas wish had come true - he was able to get the airplanes back in the air and operational again. He was helping to keep his troops protected.

When the library supervisor returned from the holidays, she was amazed at all that had transpired. She heard the story from one person, then another, and another. It had taken all of them working as a team to accomplish the feat of getting the manual out to Iraq. The process took almost 48 hours, but they were successful when others were not.

Then more thank you emails came from Iraq, other troops, other base personnel, and ultimately, the base commander. People were amazed that the library staff was able to accomplish what so many others had failed to do.

The library staff was not surprised, they were however, very satisfied that they were able to help support the troops directly. It was a great feeling!

More Satisfaction

Sometimes the satisfaction comes in a small event, but one that still makes a big impact.

At the same base, many aircraft were used as test assets, and were often one-of-a-kind types, with unique and costly equipment mixes that had to be carefully documented and tracked. The individual charged with tracking these changes often kept a binder with drawings and notes that could be quickly updated. The binder was kept right by the aircraft so that anyone making the changes had access to it. The aircraft was kept in a hangar with the latest safety equipment, including a state-of-the-art fire suppression system which extinguished flames with chemical foam.

One memorable day, the hangar fire extinguisher system was accidentally triggered by an electrician. The extinguisher quickly foamed the entire hangar bay. The repair was made quickly but the foam remained on the hangar floor, the plane, and the table holding the only binder with all the aircraft's test information. The foam was allowed to subside and the damage assessed. Fortunately, the aircraft could be cleaned, and no permanent problems were found, but every page in the binder was damaged. Attempts to dry it made it worse. Then, someone remembered that the library had dealt with wet documents before, when a basement flooded. Perhaps they had a solution. The library did.

The library worked with a conservation facility which had drying chambers used to preserve wet books. The library called and began an emergency pickup and delivery for the binder. The process involved library staff coming in after hours and on weekends, but they complied. The binder was quickly returned from the facility – at no charge because of their previous connection. It was not unscathed, but it was preserved and the text, illustrations, and change notes were readable. By the time the aircraft was ready to operate, the binder was again available to track its changes, at no cost. Another, small but worthwhile success for the library, and another satisfaction.

Sierra View Library, Reno, NV – S. Bradley

'Come, Watson, come!' he cried. 'The game is afoot. Not a word! Into your clothes and come!'

Sherlock Holmes

CHAPTER 45 -**CHALLENGE**

A reference librarian in a technical library received this email challenge from one of her scientist patrons. He had a lot of knowledge but perhaps less common sense. Names have been changed to protect the innocent. P = patron.

In 1967, this fellow claimed that he could etch sapphire with a gas that I have plumbed into my etch chamber. I'm not seeing any results. Any chance you could find this obscure journal?

H. M. Manasevit and F. L. Morritz, <u>This Journal</u>, 114, 204 (1967)

1. Thanks,
2. P

I am on it. The game's afoot.

Librarian

Crazy. I found another article in the same journal that looks really interesting. Would you look for both of these for me?

3. Thanks,
4. P
5. #2

A. Reisman, M. Berkenblit, J. Cuomo, and S.A. Chan, <u>This Journal,</u> 11S, 1653 (1971).

From: Librarian
To: P
Subject: RE: A challenge! #2

Good Morning P,
The real crazy question is - where did you get these citations?

I have attached the articles.

Hope I found the correct articles. Please let me know if I can be of further assistance!

Librarian

To: Librarian
From: P
Subject: RE: A challenge! #2

These are fantastic!

I found these citations in a 70's paper posted on the web. I've never heard of a journal called "this journal". What a horrible name! Looks like the articles are pretty good despite the bad name.

Thanks so much.

P

From:	Librarian
To:	P
Subject:	RE: A challenge! #2

Well—my guess is that the paper you found on the web was from the <u>Journal of the Electrochemical Society</u> as are the papers I just sent - so the author cited the papers as being in "this journal" meaning the same journal.

Have a great week!

■ ■

From:	P
To:	Librarian
Subject:	RE: A challenge! #2

Ah Ha! Brilliant Librarian! You are TV detective good.

P

SECTION 10

PAST, PRESENT, & FUTURE

Hageman Public Library, Porter, IN – R. Pendleton

It may not seem like much, but think of the consequences. One overdue library book today, the collapse of the universe by the end of the week

Gareth Roberts

CHAPTER 46 - **OVERDUE**

According to *Guinness World Records*, the largest fine ever paid for an overdue library book is $345.14. That was the amount owed at two cents a day for the poetry book *Days and Deeds* checked out of Kewanee Public Library, Illinois, in 1955 by Emily Canellos-

Simms. Although the book was due back 19 April 1955, Emily found it in her mother's house 47 years later and presented the library with a check for overdue fines.

Why do people hold onto their library books? Sometimes they are embarrassed, sometimes they don't feel they can afford the fine. But sometimes they simply fall in love with a book and cannot bear to give it up, even when it is usually easier just to buy another copy. But that is what Thomas McArdle did.

Thomas was 12 years old in 1936 when he visited his library at Chestnut Street Elementary School, in Scottsdale, AZ. His assignment was to write a paper about a book. He chose a new book, *The Birth of Rome* by Laura Orvieto. That book changed his life. He fell in love with history, and couldn't bear to return the book, reading it three or four more times. There is no explanation of why the library didn't charge him for the missing book, but he kept it, and carried it with him for the next 73 years.

He was in the military during World War II, and moved a lot. He attended college and majored in, of course, history. He married, worked, retired, and after living in several other states, ended up in Greenbelt Maryland. In 2010 at the age of 85 he saw the book and decided to return it to the library. He had accumulated many books by then, and would never have parted with it, except to give it back to the rightful owner. I also suspect he worried about the fine.

After contacting a friend who still lived in Scottsdale, McArdle was able to mail it back to the school district. The district determined that it now belonged to the Southmoreland Middle School. Luckily, the middle school principal, Daniel Clara, loved the book's story and waived the fine. After 73 years the book completed its long journey back to the library where it all began.

It may not be as long overdue as some New York Library books reportedly borrowed by George Washington over 200 years ago. (The fine for that infraction was calculated at over $300,000.) Nor was it out as long as a book returned to Washington and Lee library after 145 years. That book was part of a set on the Napoleonic Wars. It was taken in 1864 by C. S. Gates, a private in the Union Army, when the library was looted during General Hunter's raid. Once returned, the book rejoined it's set in their special collections. If paid, the fine would have been over $50,000.

Overdue books are like running out of gas, or missing a plane – scary until it happens and you realize that the world didn't end. Most libraries tend to be forgiving, and just want the item returned. Sometimes libraries sponsor drives when all fines are forgiven, and no questions are asked. Still, we worry about the amount we might owe. Stories about long overdue books and big fines don't help.

The Library's most important contract with its clients is the agreement to return library materials on time and in the same condition as when it had been borrowed. This is because books and documents which might have been easily replaced when new can become almost irreplaceable after years in the collection. Many people believe that overdue fines bring revenue into the library. This is almost never true; usually it is simply turned over to whatever agency operates the library and disappears in the Miscellaneous category. Collecting overdue fines is as much of a nuisance as retrieving the book itself, but library administrators persist in believing that fines will Teach A Valuable Lesson.

Many books are overdue but few transform the reader's life. Thomas McArdle's book, on *The History of Rome* brought passion into young Thomas's life, and that is what librarians all wish a library book will do.

Ann Arbor, MI Library – R. Pendleton

I always tell people that I became a writer not because I went to school but because my mother took me to the library. I wanted to become a writer so I could see my name in the card catalog.

Sandra Cisneros

CHAPTER 47- **ODE TO A CARD CATALOG**

I've been wondering how long it's been since I've seen someone actually use a card catalog to locate a book. I am guessing it has been about 30 years - since the early 1980s when most libraries became automated. Initially, computer systems were unreliable and card catalogs were kept around as backups. But over time the bugs in the Online Public Access Catalog (OPAC) systems were fixed and the old card catalogs began to disappear. I've seen them in a few larger libraries like the University of Illinois Champaign-Urbana, which maintains one for older items, and in a very few smaller libraries which have not been automated. But in most libraries they are gone.

Formerly, in large libraries, the many wooden cabinets of cards occupied entire rooms and were treated reverentially as the source for locating all the books. The cabinets were usually divided into authors, subjects, and titles. In some sophisticated systems, they could include corporate authors, editors, multi-layered subjects, and other categories that were necessary depending upon the nature of the library. One universally important use was as a shelf list, e.g., a list of every item on the shelves in that particular library.

As they were no longer used, something had to be done with them. The old wood cabinets were quickly grabbed up and recycled into a variety of new uses. I've heard and seen them used to house CDs, nuts and bolts, tools, small toys, old checks or letters, baseball cards, and other craft and hobby pieces. People happily turned them into large sewing kits, storage for fishing flies and lures, buttons, postcards,pens and

pencils,playing cards, and the like. Recently, I saw one on "The Big Bang Theory" in Sheldon and Leonard's apartment. I haven't heard of any explanation for it, but assume it is one of Sheldon's many quirks, used to control and organize his life.

Because the wood used to manufacture card catalogs is usually good quality they are often morphed into pieces of furniture. As such, they have become accent pieces, night and end tables, stands for televisions, plants, and fine art, consoles and even wine holders. Sometimes they are modified to fit the new use, or the items are modified to fit the drawers. One library (Lake Geneva, WI) wisely honors its building fund donors with plaques on permanent display in their library's now retired card catalog.

There are still adults who wander into a library and ask where the card catalog is, even if they suspect it may be a computer, but most GEN Y or younger folks have never used one. Most have probably never seen one. The wooden cabinets full of drawers are part of the pre-computer age of typewriters, carbon papers, White-out, and mimeograph machines.

One memory of card catalogs I have was while working in a large (million volume plus) academic library with a staff of about a dozen semi-professional staffers who were trusted to file the cards. Twice a week for two hours at a time we stood in front of the drawers and filed. It was a tedious job taking many staff hours. The cards were left above the rod, only to be dropped by the professional librarians who checked the work. A card once permanently filed was only removed if the book was lost or weeded and not replaced.

A kind of camaraderie formed as we filed the cards. Bits of knowledge and trivia were shared. " Hey we've got _" when a new best seller had been received. "Did you know that Babe Ruth's real name was George Herman Ruth?" "Does it matter if the subject is in all caps?" We had to concentrate on the task, but became comfortable enough over time to confide personal information too. It was an opportunity to share news about boyfriends, girlfriends, spouses, and children.

That was where we learned that Emma was going to retire – after 35 years, and we thought she would be there forever. We discussed the plans for food and games at Carla's wedding shower. We heard of Susan's acceptance to law school, and first saw Debbie's engagement ring. Sadly, we found out that Margaret's cancer had returned, and she never returned to work – She was only 28. Her funeral was a few months later. Filing at the card catalog we were able to relax and appreciate each other's company. We learned to value that time and to value each other.

My one regret is that I was not wise enough to get a card catalog when I had the chance. After many years, our library had determined that it made no sense to hold on to the relic and had put several out where they were to be sold at auction. Slowly but surely they disappeared. Several people stopped by the building to ask if there would be more available. Everyone recognized that they were useful and beautiful items. If you check on the internet today there may be some in different sizes available in good condition for prices varying from $200-$2000. I do not have one, but I will always remember them.

Hyannis, MA Public Library – J. Wu

A book is a fragile creature, it suffers the wear of time, it fears rodents, the elements and clumsy hands. So the librarian protects the books not only against mankind but also against nature and devotes his life to this war with the forces of oblivion.

Umberto Eco

CHAPTER 48 – **BOOK MARKS**

Library staff are used to finding an odd assortment of materials used by patrons to mark the pages of books so that they may find their place again. Patrons often forget that they have left them in their books, or they see them but don't have time or energy to remove them when books are returned. Sometimes items accidentally slip into the books. Staff try to find them in time to return them to the owner, as the lost and found box is usually already full. The bookmarks are a sign of how creative and or desperate we are. Here is a list of reported items.

Writing materials/papers

Envelopes – blank and empty or addressed and full (We usually mail these if it appears that that was the intent. I recently received a Christmas card (This was in May) with a notation in different ink and handwriting that indicated it had been "Found in a library book."

Letters
Postcards
Address labels
Emails
Magazine inserts
Shopping lists
Sketches, pictures, coloring book pages
Wrapping paper, newspaper, or bags
Origami
Bank/ATM receipts
Checks, or deposit slips
Money – sometimes when a patron wants to pay fine for an overdue, sometimes a larger bill or check.
Recipes
Patterns – clothing, knitting
School papers
Store receipts

Playing cards
Score sheets
Bridge talleys

Fabric and clothing
Gloves, mittens
Pieces of fur
Doll clothes
Socks
Nylon hose
Hats
Rain hats
Handkerchiefs

Neckwear
Scarves
Necklaces
Lanyards
Bandanas
Collars (for dogs or cats)

Personal grooming items
Emery boards
Combs
Folding brushes
Eyebrow pencils

Toys
– usually small and plastic
Cars, trucks, motorcycles
Soldiers, police, firemen, cowboys and Indians
Dolls with or without clothing or hair

Paper dolls
Yoyo and kite string,
kite tails
tiny kites

Food and food-related items
Candy and gum wrappers
Chip and snack bags
Licorice
Gummy worms and gummy fish
Stick candy
Peppermint
Pieces of dried fruit

The Great Outdoors
Leaves
Twigs
Seed packets
Flowers – dried or fresh – some artificial
Snake skin,
and a raccoon tail

Reno, NV Public Library – S. Bradley

New Laws of Librarianship:

Libraries serve humanity.
Respect all forms by which knowledge is
        communicated.
Use technology intelligently to enhance service.
Protect free access to knowledge.
Honor the past,
and create the future.

Michael Gorman, *American Libraries* 9/95

CHAPTER 49 – **TECHNOLOGY**

One of my strangest memories was hearing from a library visitor who sadly told me how sorry he would be when the library closed. For it certainly could not exist for more than another 10 years or so now that everything was on the Internet. That was at least 25 years ago. Of course, we know that not everything is on the Internet, nor is it all free. Librarians often hear that their days are numbered, but we have good answers for it. I'm not going to list the ways we add value, because readers know we organize and provide access to the online and physical collections. But the concept still requires thought.

The many resources available at our fingertips with a WIFI connection, or a smart phone enrich our lives. Libraries have greatly benefitted from the ability to provide their collections to their patrons who can now read and research, find, request and renew almost anywhere. We live in a golden age where technological growth enables us to do more with ease.

That also creates a dilemma. Technology allows us to provide a great deal, but budgets prevent us from supplying everything to everyone. Libraries have always had to make tough decisions on what they select for their patrons, and on what to provide in hard copy or digital – or in both formats. It is a constant struggle to make tougher decisions as technology grows exponentially.

So it comes as no surprise that some of us are concerned that the book we know might disappear. That has prompted many to fight back with arguments to save the book. (One favorite is the argument posed in *It's a Book* by Lane Smith.) Even so, with budget crises at federal, state, and local levels, it has been a tough sell. But most of us view books as works of art. We recognize that the font, the design, the photographs, and illustration can be beautiful . We luddites will fight to keep it.

The book as art is appreciated on many levels. Collectors, readers, and artists, all understand what those who create books are doing – making something of value. Indeed books are art, like sculptures and paintings. So I, and many others, believe that the book will continue to be published and treasured by generations to come for its artful beauty, in addition to the wonderful ideas, stories, or information it may provide.

In the words of a friend, the librarian and blogger, Julie Cornett:

A book is an article of warmth and beauty, attributes that electronic resources can aspire to, yet the gap is great. Books have texture, and as they age, develop a scent of their own-- something one will hope never happens to their Ipad or Kindle. Holding and paging through a book is a sensual experience. Books have their very own personalities, and the best are works of art, with sumptuous covers (the recent *Telegraph Avenue*, by Michael Chabon, has a silver hard cover that actually feels similar to a shiny, slick vinyl record, one of the key plot components) and pages that are warm and soft, like skin, often with beautiful images printed into them. To me a book feels more *real* than an electronic source…the same way a beautiful LP record feels more real than an MP3 file, downloaded from a faceless online entity.

Belle Cooledge Library, Sacramento, CA – S. Bradley

Libraries are reservoirs of strength, grace and wit, reminders of order, calm and continuity, lakes of mental energy, neither warm nor cold, light nor dark. The pleasure they give is steady, unorgastic, reliable, deep and long-lasting.

Germaine Greer

CHAPTER 50 – **REFLECTIONS**

At about the time I was learning to speak English, I spoke German also, talking to my German-speaking

Grandma. My father used to brag about taking four-year-old Elsa to the library where I would sit on the check-out counter and sing my German songs. It wasn't till I grew up that I did the math and realized that this was during the middle of World War II.

Librarians, and library staff in general, are patient and long-suffering. Although my father apparently never did "get it", I'm sure <u>they</u> did, and wondered what to do with this smiley but vague patron and his little blonde child and their possibly pro-Axis propaganda.

A half-dozen years later, trying to read my way through the children's department at the Lakewood, Ohio, Public Library, I got all the way to F in the fiction collection before giving up. I flunked one summer reading club because I wouldn't read a sports story (that was the year you had to read one book in each of the Dewey Decimal sections).

When, after finishing Library School with my Master's of Science proclaiming my identity as a "real" librarian, I got my first library job, I had never even seen the back rooms of a public library. On my first day, a patron asked me for a "book of brief cases." It took about an hour to learn that he was interested not in luggage but in short anecdotes about the law.

And yet I came back for the next day. And the next. And the next. And I miss the library work even today, fourteen years after leaving public library work. I miss sitting at the reference desk on a lazy summer afternoon, watching the changing shadows as the sun lights the book stack in turn. I miss the delicious gluttony of filling my arms with books I want to read myself, instead piling them in a display to tempt my patrons. I miss the crazy phone calls from the guys at the corner bar, betting on who won an obscure boxing match or which was bigger - a cubic centimeter or a square inch.

I miss the two elderly men who came every morning to study the stock market and who fought over the *Wall Street Journal*, pulling the newspaper stick back and forth. I miss the man whose pants kept threatening to fall down, as he read our telephone directories, one after the other, chuckling to himself.

A safe place for the strange, a welcoming refuge warm in winter and cool in summer, the library accepts everybody who wants to come in. Unlike schools, libraries let you come and go as you want. The staff will work hard to answer your questions, and best of them will help you tell them what you <u>really</u> want to know. They will protect your right to read what you wish, as long as you respect the ultimate Library Law: Return Your Books On Time.

May they survive. We need our libraries more than ever now, to protect the unpopular theories and the forgotten poets, to introduce our children to Mr. Toad and Narnia, and to remind our politicians that there is a need for civility that is as basic as sunlight, as necessary to the human spirit as music or truth or love.

References

American Library Association: "Library Quotes." *Ilovelibraries.org.* 2012.

Burnett, Leo: "Save the Troy Library: Adventures in Reverse Psychology." *Youtube.com*, November 15, 2011.

Bustillo, Miguel: "Library that Holds no Books." *Wall Street Journal*, February 6, 2013.

Christie, Casey: "Showcase Library to open in Frazier Park." *Bakersfield Californian*, October 16, 2011.

Cornett, Julie: "Hello 2013. I Will Write More." *www.formerlyfrontierlibrarian.wordpress.com,* Jan 7, 2013.

Doctorow, Cory: "Tiny Library raises money with tiny Uke and Awesome Video." *Boingboing.net*, March 6, 2012.

Eberhart, George M., compiler: *The Whole Library Handbook 3.* Chicago, American Library Association, 2000.

Fiacre: "The Fantastic Flying Books of Mr. Morris Lessmore." *librarybazaar.com*, January 30, 2012.

Goldberg, Albert: *Pentagon 9/11.* Washington, DC: Historical Office, Office of the Secretary of Defense, 2007.

Government Book Talk: "Losing our Shared National Experience." *govbooktalk.gpo.gov.* October 31, 2011.

Grundfest, Jill, ed.*: 200 Years in Madison County; Historical and*

Genealogical Resources in Madison County Libraries, Published on the Occasion of Madison County's Bicentennial, 2006. Utica, NY: Mid-York Library System, 2005.

Heritage Emergency National Task Force: "Cataclysm and Challenge: The Impact of September 11, 2001 on Our Nation's Cultural Heritage." Washington, DC: Heritage Preservation, 2002.

Johnson, Marilyn: *This book is overdue! How Librarians and Cybrarians can save us all.* New York: Harper, 2010.

Johnson, Marilyn: "U.S. Public Libraries: We lose them at our Peril." *Los Angeles Times,* July 6, 2010.

Kristof, Nicholas D.: "His Libraries, 12,000 So Far, Change Lives." *New York Times,* November 5, 2011.

Krugman, Paul: *Conscience of a Liberal* "In Praise of Public Libraries." *New York Times,* May 13, 2013.

Lopez, Steve: "Librarian's words are binding." *Los Angeles Times*, November 9, 2011.

Maurer, Giles: "Ellie Mobile Libraries." *elefantasia.org,* December 1, 2011.

Mudd, Sara: "Little Free Little Free Library connects local and global communities throughout 36 countries." *OCLC Next Space*, oclc.org, May 31, 2013.
Nasaw, David: *Andrew Carnegie.* New York, Penguin, 2006.

Newman, Bobbi, and Erin Downey Howerton: "This is What a

Librarian Looks Like. *"lookslikelibraryscience.com,* February 13, 2012.

Pogebrin, Robin*:"* New York Public Library Shifts Plan for 5th Ave. Building." *New York Times*, September 19, 2012.

Saint Louis, Catherine: "A Dark and Itchy Night." *New York Times,* December 5, 2012.

Smith, Lane: *It's a Book.* NY: Roaring Brook Press. 2010.

Smith, Russell C.: "How the little Free Library is Reinventing the Library." *Huffington Post,* June 21, 2012.

Smith Sonia: "Big Box Store has new Life as an Airy Public Library." *New York Times,* September 1, 2012.

Wickersham, Joan: "On the Shelves," *Boston Globe*, October 7, 2011. Joan Wickersham's column appears regularly in the Globe. Her website is www.joanwickersham.com.

Wood, John: *Leaving Microsoft to Change the World.* New York: Harper, 2006.

What you can do to help

If you've gotten to this part of the book, you understand the message. We love books and libraries. We think you do too.

So what can you do to help preserve and develop libraries for future generations? As much or as little as you like, but we hope you'll do something. Here are a few ideas.

1. Join a Friends of the Library group

2. Volunteer to help with a library program or fundraiser Ask the library staff if they need help? And do what they ask, even if it seems trivial or menial.

3. Vote for library bonds and support candidates that support libraries.

4. Use the library, borrow materials, attend the programs and encourage others to do so.

5. Donate books and funding, and tell others how much you save by using a library.

6. Buy from the library's gift shop and book sales.

Our primary goal in writing this book is to gain support. You can make an immediate difference. Buy a copy and share it with others. The total proceeds of this book will go to support libraries. No one involved is taking a cent. Tell others that you like it on blogs, Facebook, Twitter, Linked-In and other sites. Get the word out - libraries need your support.

Thank you,

Sandy and Elsa

Acknowledgements

It takes a village, or at least a lot of help. We couldn't have done it with the support of our family and friends. They did everything from providing artwork, design and photographs to editing and selecting, We want to thank our husbands, Jerry and Bob, our sisters Laura, Chris, and Debbie, and brother Jay. Special thanks to Ann Seider for her invaluable help and to all our friends who encouraged us.

The wonderful cover art was designed and painted by Don Sullivan who donated his services for the cause.

We had many contributors; some wished to remain anonymous. Here are a few in alphabetical order:

Julie Cornett
Robin Daly
Marsha Lloyd
Barbara Lupei
Ann Parham
Alice Pastorious
Jennie Paton
Justin Ray
Mary Ray
Joan Wickersham
Nancy Willard

And finally to all the librarians and staff who faithfully serve, we thank you and salute you.

About the authors

Both of the authors are of a certain age. They have the advantage of wonderful husbands, above-average children, and the most outstanding grandchildren.

During their careers, Sandy Bradley and Elsa Pendleton have worked in many kinds of libraries; academic, public, special, scientific-technical, and military. They have spent a combined total of over 80 years in the library world. They still volunteer and teach about libraries.

They love books and libraries, and share that love with others of similar tastes. That is why they are committed to giving back any monies earned by the sale of this book to libraries.

About the Libraries

You probably guessed that the photos are from libraries we have worked at, or visited during our travels, over the years. As a result, some were simply called, "littlest library" or "storefront library. " The identification of some is not exact, but many will be familiar to you. We had no idea they would someday be part of a book, and therefore some descriptions are vague. We apologize, but hope you will be able to enjoy the images for what they mean to us all.

Made in the USA
Lexington, KY
16 May 2014